The Pleasure of Being Oneself

The Pleasure of
Being Oneself

by

CYRIL E. M. JOAD

Essay Index Reprint Series

BOOKS FOR LIBRARIES PRESS
FREEPORT, NEW YORK

First Published 1951

Reprinted 1970 by arrangement with
Philosophical Library, Inc.

STANDARD BOOK NUMBER:
8369-1665-4

LIBRARY OF CONGRESS CATALOG CARD NUMBER:
74-111841

PRINTED IN THE UNITED STATES OF AMERICA

Contents

INTRODUCTION

IT was suggested to me by the enterprising publishers at whose initiative this book was undertaken, that I should write on *The Pleasures of Conversation*, a proposal which I gladly embraced. When, however, I came to consider what the pleasures of conversation were, I found that I enjoyed very few of them—on the whole I think that life would have been easier and more agreeable if most men and nearly all women had remained at the silent film stage—and that, such as they were, my enjoyment of them was common and, because common, unremarkable.

When, moreover, I proceeded to ask myself what my pleasures were, I found that most of them fell into the same category. They were common and unremarkable, and when I say "unremarkable," I do not mean that they were not worthy of remark, but merely that there was no remark to be made about them which hadn't been made many times before. Who wants to hear about the pleasures of strawberries and cream, of burgundy and brie, of roast lamb (English) and green peas (untinned), of walking over moors and mountains, of winning the fifth set at tennis or hitting a four at cricket, of a fine spring morning or of a fine winter morning with hoar-frost sparkling in the sun, of making bonfires in November, of getting into a hot bath when tired, cold and wet, of listening to Mozart quartets, of speeding departing guests, of making a successful speech or of making love ?

These pleasures, which are known to most of us—some of them to all of us—need no description. They ask only to be enjoyed. But there are some pleasures which are of a more individual kind. There are pleasures which are proper only to certain types of men—we don't all, for example, enjoy the pleasures of the torturer, the sea captain,

7

the musical composer or the homosexual—while others are peculiar to individual men. It is these last that interest me.

When you are young, you are repeatedly disconcerted at finding that some pursuit that other people appear to enjoy, sitting up late talking, for example, being festive with members of the family, going for a sail or a ride in a car, gives you no pleasure at all. (Though we are so prone to be kidded by other people into believing that we enjoy something which gives us no enjoyment, that it normally takes us a long time to wake up to the fact.) Equally disconcerting, but far more agreeable, is the discovery that we are susceptible of enjoyments that others don't share—that we derive, for example, an intense pleasure from digging, or being on a hay-rick, or sitting alone in a wood on a late October afternoon when the sun's rays slant and the still air shimmers in the haze. These, then, are pleasures peculiar to the self.

There is a fairly recognisable type of man who never quite gets over his surprise at finding himself mildly at odds with his society. He wants to be respectable and esteemed but somehow—and it is typical of him that he doesn't know how or why—society does not in fact esteem him. However hard he tries to stand well with eminent and respectable persons, his efforts meet with failure. All round him he sees men being elected, appointed, promoted, given positions of trust, emolument and distinction. . . . But nobody ever promotes or appoints him. He cannot quite forgive society for these, to him, unaccountable slights, and does his best to get his own back by joining the rebels and pulling faces. Or he snipes from a safe position behind the hedge.

But the rebellion is not very serious, the faces not very ugly, the sniping not prolonged. For on the whole he likes his fellow men, wants to be liked by them and enjoys himself pretty well, so that with the best will in the world he simply can't keep hostilities going.

To this type I belong. If I venture to recognise Socrates, Montaigne, Samuel Butler and H. G. Wells among my

spiritual ancestors, and Charlie Chaplin as my most eminent
living contemporary, I hope that I shan't be thought to
liken myself to these great men in any other respect.

It is of the pleasures, then, of this type of man, and more
particularly of an individual member of the type, that I
propose to write in this book.

C. E. M. JOAD,
Hampstead,
July, 1950.

NOTE.

My thanks are due to Mr. Thurston Dart for kindly reading through
Chapter IX, for making many valuable suggestions and for saving me from
some blunders.　He is, however, in no way responsible for the views
expressed.

CHAPTER I

The Pleasures of Mischief

Sundays at the Murrays'

I WILL begin with two early specimens of the pleasures of the self which, though in themselves unremarkable, will, hope, strike the correct note of the book ; for these earl pleasures, the pleasures, as I call them, of mischief, have, a I can now see, prolonged themselves, albeit in a chastene form and under many disguises and aliases, through most of my adult life.

To my father, an inspector of schools, there was appointe in 1902, as assistant, H. J. R. Murray, a son of Sir Jame Murray, who was at that time engaged upon the monu mental work which made him famous and won him h knighthood, the editing of the *Oxford English Dictionary*. M parents were dissatisfied with my education at the loc snob school and were looking round for a school at whic I could be given a little academic polish, be groomed i fact for a scholarship to a public school. It was Murra who suggested Lynam's Preparatory School, Oxford—th Dragon School, as it was called. (As this has since becom one of the most celebrated preparatory schools in th country, I shall say nothing about it here except that m life there was happy and normal, and that it did me a grea deal of good, for which I am properly grateful.) The speci advantage claimed for Lynam's was that it was just roun the corner, less than a couple of hundred yards from th home of Sir James and Lady Murray. They, Murra assured my anxious parents, would keep an eye on me. point of fact they did a good deal more, inviting me spend the day with them on Sundays. Sunday after Sunday for nine long terms I repaired after morning church to Sunnyfields, arriving in time for mid-day dinner, staying to tea and returning to the school about six.

The Murrays' was a large Victorian household containing in my time three unmarried daughters whose ages ranged from seventeen to twenty-five, one son then at Magdalen, and a young male cousin from South Africa. (These were only a selection from the ten or eleven children who had been born to the Murrays, the majority of whom were by now acquitting themselves with distinction in the world outside.)

The girls were jolly, cheerful and to me very kind, but homely. Their lives were bound, at any rate so far as Sunday was concerned, by a ritual that never varied. Sir James was a member of some straight Presbyterian sect, and at about ten the whole family would set off to an obscure chapel somewhere near the Union where Sir James was a pew holder. I think he also read the lessons. They returned to dinner about 12.45. At dinner there were always three or four undergraduate guests, often from the Dominions, besides the family and myself. The menu never varied. There was a large round of roast beef slightly raised from the dish, with a Yorkshire pudding spread beneath it, followed by a tart, the fruit in which varied with the season, but was usually apple. The food was plain but very good. I have never eaten better Yorkshire pudding in my life. We drank ginger wine of which I could never get enough.

At two we repaired to the drawing room where polite conversation took place. At 2.30 I and whichever younger members of the family felt so disposed were permitted to withdraw to the nursery. All the children had been brought up in this nursery and they felt at home there. Here they could mentally as well as physically unbutton. We spent the afternoon reading and eating sweets. I, being, I suppose, about twelve years old at the time, read the *Boys' Own Paper* and *Chums*. At 4.30 we went down to tea in the drawing room, where a fresh batch of undergraduates was in attendance ready for a further bout of polite conversation. At 5.45 the family departed for evening service at the chapel, and at 6 o'clock I went back to school. Such was the Sunday routine at the Murrays', and, week in, week out, it scarcely ever varied. (When I returned to Oxford some six years later as an undergraduate, I used to call at the Murrays', and the routine was still the same. There were still the two batches of lunching and tea-ing undergraduates, of whom I was now privileged to be one. The jolly daughters were perhaps a little jollier. If I remember rightly, one of the three married during my undergraduate period.) The only radical change occurred in the summer when we spent hot, somnolent afternoons in the garden instead of in the nursery. The garden contained a very large tin hut, dignified by the name of the Scriptorium, where during the week Sir James worked on the Dictionary, assisted by a considerable staff, including two of his daughters.

The Pleasure of the Horse

In one corner of the nursery stood an old rocking horse which had been used by each of the Murray children in turn. I noticed one day that its tail, a peg of wood surrounded by horsehair, was loose. When pulled sharply it came away, leaving a large hole in the horse's posterior. Lady Murray was very strict in the matter of untidy plates. Everything had to be eaten and the plate cleared, however reluctant the eater. Sprouts in those days were an abomination to me ; indeed, except when they are very young and cooked "just so" in butter, they are so still. One Sunday, unable to finish an unusually generous helping, I waited until the conversation was brisk enough to occupy everybody's attention, and surreptitiously conveyed three or four large, hard, yellow-looking brutes into my handkerchief, which I hid in my pocket. My problem was now how to dispose of the concealed sprouts. It was then that I thought of the hole in the horse's behind. Leaving the drawing room and getting into the nursery well ahead of the others, I removed the tail, shot the sprouts into the horse's belly and replaced the peg. This action afforded me a peculiar and very intense pleasure. It was not merely a convenient method of getting rid of the sprouts ; it served in some obscure way as a symbol, a symbol of protest and defiance against the decorous regularity which prevailed in the Murray household.

Lin Yutang, that admirable writer on Chinese philosophy, tells us that though the Confucian code ruled the major part of the lives of Chinese officials, counselling the decorous conduct of the good citizen anxious to do his duty, to improve his position in the State hierarchy and to stand well with the neighbours, human nature being what it is, even the best regulated Confucians are subject to occasional outbursts of indecorum. Man's spirit, it is intimated, needs from time to time to take a holiday and to "go on the spree." Taoism provides the necessary safety-valve ; it encourages a man to throw off the strait-jacket of a too rigid decorum and play the spiritual truant. "Man," says Mr. Lin Yutang, "has a hidden desire to go about with dishevelled hair which Confucianism does not quite permit. The man who enjoys slightly rebellious hair and bare feet goes to Taoism." "Taoism," he adds, "stands for revolt against the artificiality and responsibilities of urban life and Confucian culture. . . . Its political views are anarchic."

It was in something of a Taoist spirit that I proceeded to make use of the orifice left by the horse's tail. Once this receptacle for unwanted food had been discovered, and its secure convenience established, I found it difficult to hold my hand. Sunday after Sunday I collected my unwanted scraps, furtively conveyed them upstairs and gleefully shot them through the horse's bottom. Bits of gristle, little dollops of rice pudding, an occasional parsnip, bread and, of course, sprouts—all these poured through the hole. Presently the thing so grew upon me, that I used to go out of my way to collect scraps for the horse, and counted a Sunday wasted when I hadn't put something through the hole.

One day one of the daughters was heard to complain of a

curious smell in the nursery ; in spite, however, of the most careful examination, nobody could locate its origin. The smell grew and during the summer became almost unbearable. I held my peace. Something must have happened during the summer vac. to bring matters to a head or, to speak more precisely, to the tail. When I returned to school in September, the rocking horse had gone. Whether I was suspected or not I don't know, for nothing was said either to me or by me.

I find it difficult to convey the intense pleasure I took in these proceedings ; it was a secret pleasure, a private and personal pleasure, a pleasure of the self ; which brings me to the episode of the Scriptorium.

Pleasure of the Scriptorium

One Sunday in summer, for some reason that I have forgotten, the routine was broken and the family went out for the afternoon. Only Lady Murray was left in the house and, the afternoon being sultry, she slept. I was left to my own devices. For some time I prowled restlessly about the garden. Presently the Scriptorium attracted me. I had never been inside ; it would, I thought, be fun to explore. The place was locked, but after prowling round for some time I found a window ajar, prised it open and climbed in.

Round the walls were shelves full of books. Down the length of the floor ran long trestle tables, along which were ranged ink bottles, bottles of paste and gum, pens, blotting paper, numerous pairs of scissors and piles of paper covered with writing. Not much there, you would have thought, to amuse a bored boy of twelve years old. But I contrived to extract a surprising amount of entertainment from the Scriptorium. I carefully split the nibs of all the pens and overturned the bottles of ink. Over some of the piles of paper I upset the bottles of paste. Others, again, I tore up, scattering the fragments on the floor and out of the window. I opened notebooks and poured paste over their contents. I stuck drawing-pins into the backs of calf-bound volumes. I pulled books from the shelves and gummed their leaves together. One considerable bookcase I managed to pull over, scattering its contents higgledy-piggledy on the floor, upon which I proceeded to pour several wells of ink. I had a high old time ; I enjoyed myself no end.

I was subsequently told that I had delayed work on the Dictionary by at least six months. Some of the harm that I had done was irremediable. For example, there was a pile of notes by one of the editors or assistant-editors who had just died. These, which I had jumbled together and reduced to a mass of pulpy paste, were irreplaceable.

Although, once again, I held my peace, this time I was found out. There were, I believe, grave discussions as to whether I should be invited to continue my Sunday visits to Sunnyfields. But the Murrays did not like to go back on their promise to my people and the visits continued, albeit for some time I felt myself under a cloud. The reader will be pleased to hear that the matter was reported to the headmaster who beat me abundantly. Now this exploit was in its most obvious description a simple, barbarian act ; a horrid, savage little boy was demonstrating Hitler's truth that any fool can destroy in a few minutes the fabric which civilised men have taken years to build. My action was, then, as indefensible in its nature as it was disastrous in its results ; nor do I seek to defend it.

But there was more to it than that. The pleasure that I took in this exploit was more than the common pleasure of the common thug. It was also the peculiar and private pleasure of a little scallywag of an urchin, feeling in his bones that the hand of Confucian society is and ever will be against him, and anxious not to let slip the chance of getting even with it whenever opportunity offered. In this respect my pleasure was derived from and was informed by the spirit of Taoism, as Lin Yutang has defined it. While the common pleasure of the common thug evaporated quite early in my life, this private and peculiar pleasure which I have ventured to liken to the pleasures of Taoism, albeit in a tamed and watered-down form, has remained with me throughout my life.

Now that in old age, burdened with a chain of houses and flocks and herds and children and grandchildren and other impedimenta which a lifetime of industry has accreted upon and bound about me, I wear the nearest thing in the way of a likeness to a responsible person that my nature is capable of assuming, these Taoist pleasures are for the most part the pleasures of memory only, and I can meditate upon them in tranquillity. They were, then, I submit, not wholly ignoble, inasmuch as they demanded for their indulgence a willingness to take risks which the vulgar would call cheek but which, I insist, amounted on occasion to courage—the courage of the *gamin*. Behold society chewing like a comfortable cow the cud of its vast complacency. For the most part, it is dormant and takes no notice of the darts and stings administered to it by the mischievous little urchin playing round its flanks. But every now and then he takes a liberty too many, and it stirs from its torpor and turns upon and rends him with terrible effect. Yes, the pleasures of Taoism carry their element of risk. My nerve isn't what it was and my challenges to society grow rarer and feebler. Yet throughout my young adult life I made them with some confidence and frequency. I will give one more example.

The Death of the Peacock

In the hopeful days of the early twenties—in 1920, it may have been, or 1921—a group of aspiring thinkers, economists, sociologists, social workers or socialists *tout court*, used to gather for weekend and summer schools at Dunford House, near Midhurst. Dunford House, which had once belonged to Cobden, had recently been purchased by the London School of Economics for use as a conference house, but anybody who had any connection with what for short I will call "the intellectual left" could stay there, and it was open to such bodies as the Fabian Society for their conferences and schools. The fees were moderate and the place comfortable. There was a large garden adorned by a highly decorative peacock, in which members of the conferences disported themselves or took their rest, and the country was enchanting. This was my first introduction to the country round Midhurst which has subsequently played so large a part in my life, and I was a frequent visitor.

At this period of my life I was for no assignable reason subject to noisy nightmares. At least I suppose there must have been nightmares, because of the noise that I was led to make in my sleep ; yet it was very rarely that on waking up I retained any recollection of the dream that had presumably disturbed me. But there was no doubt that I made a most horrible din. Not only did everybody assure me that this was so, but I could corroborate from the evidence of my own senses, since I used to wake to find myself standing in the middle of the room, yelling at the top of my voice and with the sound of yells past and present ringing in my ears. Indeed, it was the terrible noise I made that had woken me up. Sometimes I yelled so loudly that I abraded my vocal cords ; my throat ached, and next morning for some hours I would be voiceless.

On a certain weekend one fine spring a number of us had gathered at Dunford House. The company was distinguished, including two or three Cabinet Ministers to be. I remember the presence of Sidney, but not of Beatrice Webb. Some time in the early hours of Sunday morning I had one of my most clamant nightmares, and woke up to find myself screaming at the top of my voice near the bedroom door. I crept shamefacedly back to bed, hoping that nobody had heard me. But they had. Presently the sounds of doors opening, of hushed voices and pattering feet made themselves heard in the corridor, growing louder as they approached the door of my room. I lit a candle—electric light had still to come to Dunford House—opened the door and walked boldly into the passage. A considerable number of persons in every variety of night attire had already gathered there and more kept appearing. I particularly remember a vision of Sidney Webb, candlestick in hand and tasselled nightcap on head, wearing a nightgown. I remember how thin his shins looked as they protruded below the nightgown.

B   17

Somebody suggested burglars, the screams being presumed to be those of the burgled person. The suggestion caught on and we decided to search the house. There was some difficulty in finding leaders for the party of exploration, since it was considered not unlikely that the burglar was still in the house and might possibly be armed. Nobody, in fact, seemed to want to go first. I showed great boldness, and acquired considerable kudos by my readiness to take the lead and by the intrepidity with which I led the way into room after room with a long retinue of nervous people behind me. I pulled out drawers, opened cupboards and even peered under beds. When at last we retired I was considered to have shown great courage. The affair had an unfortunate sequel. No burglar having been discovered, the mysterious screams were attributed to the peacock. It was held that no bird should be permitted to disturb the rest of distinguished guests and he was quietly made away with. When I heard about this, I was very sorry. But if the question were put to me, would I, had I been apprised beforehand of what was intended, have spoken up to save the poor bird's life, I am afraid the answer must be "no." It was not so much a feeling of shame in regard to my nightmare yelling, for which, after all, I could not be held accountable, that would have held me back, as an unwillingness to disclose and surrender my secret pleasure, that very private and personal pleasure which I had had in leading Sidney Webb and the rest up the garden path of the Dunford House corridors.

CHAPTER II

The Pleasures of Culture

Tiverton in 1909

I DERIVED, I must suppose, a certain pleasure from reading great classical literature in the Sixth at Blundell's, but it was mild—very mild. I was at best a second-rate classical scholar, and do not remember to have been moved by the content of the literature I so laboriously learned to construe. The plays of the Greek dramatists, I remember, bored me beyond measure. Plato now—that is another matter ; but Plato was not yet. For the rest, I evinced in my school days no original literary sympathies, I developed no independent reading tastes.

My first practice of the arts of public speech and the resultant domination for two years of the School Debating Society, coupled with the performance of the star *rôles* in the school plays—these, no doubt, afforded experiences as pleasing as they were intense. There was the pleasure of self-display, the pleasure of gratified vanity, the pleasure of basking in the unaccustomed lustre of popular esteem. Great these pleasures undeniably were, civilised they emphatically were not. They were the pleasures of the actor, the tub thumper, the revivalist preacher, but not of the civilised man.

Nor, as yet, were my feelings for nature awakened. The birds-nesting, fire making, tree climbing phase was over and nothing had as yet come to take their place. . . .

My first taste of civilised pleasures came, not directly through any orthodox or premeditated channel, but accidentally, as it were, arising out of activities designed to achieve very different ends, designed in fact to cure my lisp and to teach me how to play the piano.

The need to cure my lisp made itself felt in connection with my acting. I couldn't pronounce my "s's" which sounded like "th's," and I couldn't roll my "r's." Hence arose a demand for a teacher of elocution who would rectify my deficiencies in these respects.

By what means Miss Hall was found I do not know. Tiverton in 1909 was as tucked away a little town as could be found anywhere in England. Nothing had happened there for decades, not in fact since Palmerston had represented the place in Parliament and bequeathed his name to the leading hotel. With the exception of a small lace factory, the town was given over entirely to the needs and uses of agriculture. Corn chandlers and agricultural implement makers abounded, and on market days Tiverton was a centre for farmers from many miles round. There were two restaurants—we knew them as teashops—where you could get Devonshire cream with your tea and ices in the summer. The only distinctive form of diet was a sort of doughy scone called a "Chudleigh," which we used to split down the middle preparatory to spreading the two halves with cream and jam. Of culture there was none. There was no theatre, no opera house, no debating society and no literary society. Many culturally dead towns boasted and still boast a thing called a philosophical society whose members devote themselves to mildly observing local fauna and studying local antiquities ; but at Tiverton there was not even that.

Owing to the overwhelming predominance of the Tory interest there was no political activity ; nor had there need to be. In the School Debating Society of some sixty odd boys I was one of the three Liberals (the other two were the sons of Liberal M.P.s, and because of their abhorred parentage a bad time they had of it.) I became a Liberal by some cerebral process now forgotten, but certainly unassisted, of my own, and when, as a member of the Sixth, I was made free of the town, used to sneak furtively into a news-agent's in Tiverton and emerge with a feeling of mingled insecurity, distinction, depravity and defiance with that revolutionary, class-conscious organ, the *Daily News*, then working itself up into a great heat of enthusiasm on the subjects of the Lloyd George budget and free trade. The place, I repeat, was a cultural vacuum in which the mind of man was as nearly asleep, his spirit as nearly atrophied, as it is possible for them to be this side of the grave and—for all I know to the contrary—beyond it, which makes the phenomenon of Miss Hall all the more surprising.

Phenomenon of Miss Hall

Miss Hall lived in a small house in a back street with her invalid father, and described herself on a brass plate screwed to the door as a "Teacher of Music and Elocution." I remember her as a plump woman of about fifty, with a very red face and podgy hands—the fingers rather like sausages —clothed formidably in a bodice of rusty black that came up over her neck, fortified with beads of jet and hung with gold or gilt ornaments, through whose encasing bonds her lush body seemed perpetually on the point of breaking. The general effect was sombre, plain and rich—or so it seemed to me.

I used to go to Miss Hall about half past three of an afternoon for an hour's lisp eradication. What happened about the lisp eradication I cannot remember—very little, I imagine, as the lisp is with me still. Miss Hall's method was to set me to read or recite a poem, while she sat by on the look-out for slurred "s's" and "r's." But the ostensible purport of my reading and reason for my presence were forgotten almost from the outset in the spell of the poetry or —to be accurate—in the excitement of histrionic declamation. This swept us both like a passion.

The poem which was chosen for my declamatory exercises was Poe's *The Raven*, and, incited thereto by Miss Hall, I imparted to my recitation a sinister significance which was as foreign to my nature as we deemed it to be proper to the poem. Miss Hall made me learn the thing by heart, and then declaim it striding about the room. As I enunciated those euphonious but threatening syllables, my eyes flashed, my hands gesticulated and my voice rumbled like distant thunder—although my "r's" unfortunately did not roll with my voice.

> "Prophet!" cried I, "thing of evil!—prophet still if bird or devil!—
> Whether tempter sent, or whether tempest tossed thee here ashore,
> Desolate, yet all undaunted, on this desert land enchanted—
> On this home by Horror haunted—", and so on.

How I thundered it out!

And then the last verse,

> "And the Raven, never flitting, still is sitting, still is sitting
> On the pallid bust of Pallas, just above my chamber door;
> And his eyes have all the seeming of a demon's that is dreaming,
> And the lamp-light o'er him streaming throws his shadow on the floor;
> And my soul from out that shadow that lies floating on the floor
> Shall be lifted—nevermore."

How beautifully I dropped my voice to it, so that it seemed as if with the dying away of the storm of emotion by which the poem had been swept, I, the reciter, too was fading out. How gloatingly I lingered over "His eyes have all the seeming of a demon's that is dreaming". With what unction I croaked out that last "nevermore." It was a treat to hear me.

The whole thing was very moving—very moving and affecting indeed. I enjoyed that poem, or rather I enjoyed reciting it, more than I can say. It was my first purely personal and private æsthetic experience, something whose significance I had, as it were, found for myself.

Schumann

When the excitement of the recitation had subsided, we

had tea prepared by Miss Hall's own hands in advance of my coming, for the little maid who came in the morning went at midday. I remember Chudleighs and Devonshire cream with gooseberry jam as the predominating features. After tea I would ask Miss Hall to play the piano. As the notion that women could play otherwise than on the concert platform—play domestically, as it were—was new in my experience, she must in the first instance have suggested it herself. But afterwards it became part of the recognised ritual of the afternoon that I should ask her. I can remember her playing only one composer, Schumann, and one piece by that composer, Arabesque—or, if, as I suppose, there may be several Schumann Arabesques, one of them and that the best known—for, little as I know of Schumann's music, I must have heard it dozens of times since. She played with brio and great flourishing gestures, so that I who, with the exception of Mr. Haddock's playing about to be described, had never heard a solo pianist, thought her very fine indeed. When I come to think of it, I suppose that the spiritual world of Schumann is not very different from that of Poe. Both men are lush, rhetorical and undisciplined, fabricators of vast amorphous masses of words and sounds shot through with occasional gleams of beauty, much as the smoke of a sulky autumnal bonfire may burst every now and then into a clear momentary flame. It is as though a great mass of rubbish which normally acts as an impediment or inhibition were every now and then burned through and allowed inspiration—no more than a flash, but genuine enough while it lasts—to come to the top. Then the gardener, whoever he may be, piles on more leaves and all is smoke again ; that thick left hand of Schumann's is thumping away in the bass and Poe's perpetual stream of dark-sounding words suggestive of dreams and melancholy is nattering away about funerals, bones, worms and charnel houses :—

"I dwelt alone
In a world of moan
And my soul was a stagnant tide."

The words might be from a poem by Mrs. Leo Hunter. Yet

at the time I thought Poe very fine, as I did Schumann, both of them symbolising for me worlds of experience and ranges of feeling which lay outside the confines of such culture as Blundells knew, with its circumspect references to the more decorous aspects of strictly classical art.

Mr. Haddock

In my last year at Blundell's my parents thought it would be nice if I learned to play the piano. Whether they were instigated thereto by me or whether they reached this conclusion unassisted, I cannot now remember. The music master at the School, who also played the organ in chapel, was Mr. Haddock. He was a little man with a blonde moustache, reddish hair and a face which was the colour of old bricks, and he had been there from the beginning of time. A bachelor, he lived in digs not far from the school, and he smelled faintly but perpetually of whisky. (He was, though naturally I didn't know this at the time, a confirmed alcoholist who some years later died of drink.) I suppose that Haddock had been teaching English public school boys, whom nature intended for anything in the world rather than for music, to play the piano ever since he or anybody else could remember. At any rate he had long lost interest in them.

He made no bones whatever about teaching me. One lesson was enough for him. Deciding, I suppose, from a glance at my hands, or for whatever reason, that I would never make a pianist, or, as is more probable, deciding simply that he didn't want to be bothered with me, he would set me down at the piano, tell me to practise and go off— as I now suppose—for a whisky and soda. At any rate I wouldn't see him again for half an hour or so, when he would return, ask to hear me play my one piece, and then dismiss me well within the hour.

One day, instead of dismissing me, he asked me if I would like to hear him play. Naturally I said yes, and for twenty minutes or so he played instead of me. One day in a burst of frankness he made me a little speech. "You know," he said in effect, "you won't make a pianist, no, not if you practise all day long until you live to be a hundred. The most you will achieve is the playing of a few pieces so badly that, if you have any music in you, you won't be able to endure listening to yourself. If you haven't, why bother anyway ? But I will tell you what you can do ; you can learn to listen. It isn't everybody who can do that, mostly because they didn't have the chance of it when they were young. Now here's your chance. I will play for you if you like, and you can listen."

What boy could resist such an invitation ? It wasn't so much the lure of music, which meant little to me at that time, as the sheer fun of "getting out of" something, that made the proposal irresistible. The fact that my father was paying so much an hour for the lessons and naturally expected something to show or, rather, to hear for his money, meant nothing to me.

I said that I would like to listen—"having your taste formed" was what Haddock called it—and thereafter two or three times a week after morning school he would play to me (after a couple of whiskies) from twelve to one.

He played for the most part overtures, overtures whose names are familiar—or were then—even when their composers are forgotten. I recall the overtures to *Tancredi*, *Semiramide*, *Masaniello*, *Raymond*, *The Barber*, *Carmen*, and above all *Zampa*, which with its rushing phrases, gradually increasing in tempo and widening in range like ripples when a stone is thrown into a pond, particularly excited me. I would hum it, whistle it, sing it and jig about all over the room in time to it.

At first, the overtures were played as solos ; then, as the procedure became recognised and established, Haddock brought in a musical boy and they played them together as duets. Haddock, I believe, enjoyed them almost as much as I did. His palpable enjoyment is not my only reason for supposing that his taste must have been pretty bad. He used to practise a good deal on the chapel organ and induced me to go and blow for him. A new organ had recently been installed, and the thing was like a toy to him ; he was always at it. Or, rather, he was at it as often and for as long as he could get a blower. I can still remember two or three of the melodies—there was always a very distinct melody—that he affected. They are of a revolting sentimentality. There was also an arrangement of Liszt's *Liebestraume* for the organ. . . . Haddock was, I remember, particularly addicted to the *vox humana* stop. And was there not also a *vox angelica*? I think that there was.

Now, I don't want to imply that whatever I may have obtained in the way of æsthetic experience from Miss Hall, or from Haddock was of a high order. It obviously was not. But it was probably the nearest thing to beauty which at that age (16–18) I was capable of taking in.

On Beauty

Moreover, as I have said, these experiences were unpremeditated. If beauty had been presented to me officially, as it were, with all the authority of the headmaster reading Shakespeare and proving it to have been written by Bacon, or of a visiting lecturer on art complete with lantern slides of "the world's best", or of the College choir behind it, some nonconformist element in me would probably have kept my senses sealed.

Even then I had learned to be on my guard against being kidded into thinking that I liked something that I didn't like merely because most people, or important people, told me that I ought to like it or assumed that I did like it. But in these two instances beauty came to me in so unassuming a guise, came so casually and unexpectedly while I and everybody about me was busy thinking about something else, that she effected her entrance unperceived, slipping into and through my still unawakened senses while the main faculties of my being were occupied elsewhere— in learning not to lisp, or in currying favour with the master by listening to his piano playing, or by blowing for him at the organ.

But, on reflection, perhaps beauty comes to everybody

like that. Looking back over my life, I can see that the music
that has moved me most has been music that was not so
much heard as overheard streaming out through the open
window of a lamplit room in which somebody was playing
a Chopin Nocturne. Or I have been surprised by the
strains of a mandolin or guitar coming over still water on a
summer night. For beauty is not a house that can be built
by men's hands, but a song that you hear as you pass the
hedge, rising suddenly into the night and dying down
again. If it is all laid on and laid out waiting for you and
you go expecting to find it, something misses fire. You
should never take a basket if you want to find mushrooms.

And so perhaps these pleasures which I enjoyed when I
was being surprised into my first æsthetic experiences, only
recognised long afterwards for what they were, were not so
personal, not so peculiar to the self as I have supposed.

Bab Ballads

One other that belonged to the same period was highly
personal. We sat down to school tea at six o'clock. It
was an austere affair—thick bread and butter and jam
garnished every now and then with a sausage or a herring.

I enjoyed for a short time the friendship of one whose
soul craved for the smart world, whose spiritual home was
"Society." He did the best he could for himself, poor
chap, at that unpromising age in these unpromising
surroundings, by giving little teas at 4.30 of an afternoon in
his study. There were a white lace table cloth, a shaded red
lamp and little chocolate cakes in frills. And there, during
the last year of my school life, two or three times a week I
would foregather of an afternoon to taste the delights of
"Society," talking school scandal and reading aloud from—
of all surprising works—the Bab Ballads. What dictated
this curious choice I don't know. Gilbert was merely a name
to me and I had yet to see my first Gilbert and Sullivan
opera. I am not particularly addicted to humorous verse
and nobody could maintain that the Bab Ballads are beautiful. However, we read them assiduously and with enormous

THE PLEASURE OF BEING ONESELF

enjoyment. My particular favourite I remember was the comparatively unknown *Emily, John, James and I*. We told ourselves that this was indeed culture. For me, at least, as I rapturously declaimed :

> "And all the people noticed that the engine of the law
> Was far less like a hatchet
> Than a dissipated saw."

This was a personal pleasure, a peculiar pleasure, a pleasure of the self.

CHAPTER III

The Pleasures of Official Baiting

IT ISN'T a good chapter title, for I want to speak of so much more than it covers. Also few officials are here baited. Yet I use it for want of a better. What I want to write about is the pleasure I have had in "getting away with it" under the nose of authority—the word "nose" being interpreted in a wide sense to cover the laws, rules, regulations, prohibitions and disapprovals both spoken and unspoken, with which authority seeks to protect and inflate itself—tweaking the organ, if possible, in the process. I put my head in the lion's mouth and the jaws fail to close ; I find a hole in the fence and pass through it. The pleasure, that of the schoolboy who plunders the orchard unscathed, is distinct and intense. I have pulled the nose of authority and "got away with" something uncovenanted. Only for a time, of course, for sooner or later I am observed, the jaws snap, the hole in the fence is filled up, the fence itself is heightened and barbed, and I have to look round for other ways of scoring. The winning of these small battles in the perpetual war which my kind wages against authority has afforded some of the most distinctive pleasures of my life, pleasures private and personal, pleasures of the self. Enjoying them, I have the feeling not merely of "saving" but of "winning" face, and laying up for myself a store of merit in—but, alas, I don't know where it is laid.

Let me give some examples.

Heinz's Baked Beans

Here is an early specimen. When Heinz's baked beans first burst upon the world, they were a gastronomic revelation. That sharp tomatoey taste, blending in perfect harmony with the blandness and suavity exuded by the bean when you crunch it, provided one of those heaven-sent combinations of flavours of which ham and eggs, lamb and new potatoes and mint sauce, burgundy and brie, grilled ham and peas, raspberries and Devonshire cream, are more patent and familiar examples. I first met them at the Wolverhampton Exhibition in 1900 or 1901. Arranged in little saucers, five or six to a saucer, they were being distributed hot and gratis from the Heinz stall to all comers. The stall was in the crowded Hall of Industry and Commerce, and at most hours of the day a line of expectant applicants queued and passed before it. During many of these hours the line included myself. I considered the beans so delicious that having enjoyed my portion I slipped round the back of the stall and rejoined the tail end of the queue. In this way I would partake of a dozen or more helpings of the beans. After a time my manœuvre was spotted, and the officials behind the counter were very angry. It served their purposes in any event but ill that the beans should be consumed by a small boy whose buying potential was presumably nil, but that the small boy should come for more and come not once but again and again—that, indeed, was hard to bear. But what could they do? There they stood, clad in the robes of hospitality and benevolence, showering the contents of their horn of plenty upon all comers. It would hardly do to make exceptions, to impose limits, to suggest cheese-paring—still less to have had a row in front of the stall.

And so for several delighted hours, when the pleasures of bean-eating were enhanced by my first taste of the pleasures of official baiting, I got away with it. In parenthesis, oh that the beans had retained their pristine freshness. But that exquisite flavour has long departed. Nothing remains as it was ; everything declines from its first golden age nor, once having declined, does it ever recover. (Compare the contemporary case of frozen peas that burst for a time so gloriously upon our world not long after the war).

Paddington Station

One summer's day in 1945 I had an engagement to open

a Youth Hostel near Brent, on the southern edge of Dartmoor. The idea was that I was to mount a horse at Brent Station, ride some miles to the hostel and be photographed (a) *en route* (b) on arrival and (c) performing the opening ceremony, by *Picture Post* to whom the occasion appealed as being picturesque—"Youth goes to the country," "Hikers in shorts," "Leafy Devonshire lanes," or, alternatively, "The wide open spaces of the moor," "Joad on his horse," and so on. . . . Oddly enough, though many were taken, no pictures of Joad and the horse appeared. It was a very hot day and, on arrival, I insisted on bathing in the fast-flowing stream which ran in front of the hostel. There were rocks, rapids and deep pools of jet black water. Who could resist it ? For one of those inscrutable reasons known only to journalists, "Joad bathing"—albeit, so far as I remember, clad in a perfectly normal and, indeed, rather generous costume—appealed to the paper more than "Joad on horseback," and *Picture Post* appeared with a series of lavish photographic variations on the theme of "Joad takes a dip." It was on a Saturday afternoon that I left London, and the battle of Paddington was at its height. The station was surrounded by a mob of people, and it was only after I had clamorously insisted that I already had a seat—somebody, I swore, was actually sitting in one for me—that my taxi was allowed to approach the station at all. There were still twenty minutes before my train left, but to my dismay the gates of the platform at which it stood were closed.

I did not want to let the Youth Hostel people down ; I didn't want to disappoint *Picture Post* ; above all, I didn't want to disappoint myself. I was looking forward to the occasion, and I knew that unless I succeeded in getting on to the train, I should miss it. It was a time for heroic measures. Outside the iron gates leading to the platform stood a group of high officials fresh and cool and pink—coats buttoned up, boots shining, gold braid on their peaked hats, very stately and grand ! The Brains Trust *furore* had only recently passed its zenith and my face and general appearance were still widely known. One of the officials recognised me.

"Here," he said, "comes Professor Joad. Afternoon, Sir ! "
"Yes," I said, "and he's got to get on to that train." "Quite
impossible," replied the official in chief, "stuffed tight as
sardines they are, and locked up long ago." "Couldn't you
find room for just one ? " They shook their heads.   I
searched anxiously in my mind for some compelling pretext.
The election campaign had just begun. "I am going," I
said, "to address an election meeting in Plymouth." That
made them prick up their ears. "Oh, you are, are you ? "
said the chief official. He looked at me hard. "Which
party ? " Remembering that my own views were almost
certainly known and that it would be useless anyway to say
"Tory"—besides, I didn't think that I could have said "Tory"
—I took a deep breath and a shot in the dark : "Labour, of
course," said I.

The head official smiled, the gates were opened and I
went through, to the discomfiture and loudly expressed
annoyance of the people in the queue. I was, of course,
delighted to have caught the train, but what gave an added
edge to my pleasure was the reflection that I had bamboozled
an official.

Fabian Summer School

The Fabian Society, when I first knew it, was a very
different affair from what it has since become. It was
numerically small, politically unimportant and served as a
magnet to attract all the cranks and oddities who, for whatever reason, were in revolt against the conventions of
Edwardian middle class society. There were vegetarians,
simple lifers, nudists, abolitionists of capital punishment and
anti-vivisectionists ;   there were also advanced sexual
thinkers, those who wanted abortion legitimised, homosexuality legitimised, illegitimate children legitimised,
divorce made easy, cheap and honourable for all, and so on ;
there were even some advanced sexual doers. The Society
had, however, retained from its origin a strong streak of
puritanism, and those who ran it were very properly determined that its political effectiveness should not be compro-

32

mised by the sexual irregularities of some of its members.

The strains and stresses resulting from these divergent tendencies came to a head at the annual summer schools where Miss Hankinson, a person of strong and likeable personality but rigid morals, managed us all for our good. I was constantly in hot water for one dereliction or another. Usually, they were mild enough ; I cut a lecture to go out in a boat with a girl or came in with another after ten o'clock at night. This was lower middle class England in 1914, and my reputation suffered. A little later I spent a weekend with one of the girls from the school. We were observed and reported on, and a ban was placed upon my attendance at future schools.

I was at the time a member of a body called the Fabian Nursery. It was intellectually "larky" and morally vagabond, and it was constantly at loggerheads with the parent body which subsequently disbanded it. The Fabian Nursery was entitled to elect from its numbers one member of the Committee that organised and ran the summer school. I induced them to elect me. I was now a member of the organising and governing body of the institution that I was not entitled to attend. The resulting situation confronted the officials with a grave dilemma. Either they refused to accept the Nursery representative, thus putting up the backs of the Nursery, or they removed their ban and permitted me to attend the school, which meant climbing down and loss of face, or they retained it and precipitated a ridiculous situation on the summer school committee. Not to put too fine a point on it, they were in an awful hole. What happened is another story and a long one. It is sufficient for my present purpose, which is to illustrate by examples what I mean by official-baiting, to relate the incident and to recall the pleasure that I derived from it.

Kant and Universalisation

I am, of course, well aware that the pleasure that I have derived from baiting, bamboozling and throwing dust in the eyes of officials is not what a strict morality would approve. It offends, for example, against Kant's universalisation maxim, "Act only according to that maxim which you can at the same time will to be a universal law." In other words, don't make exceptions in your own favour. It is pretty clear that in the matter of the Heinz beans and the Paddington barrier it is precisely this that I was doing. If everybody were to partake of unlimited saucers of hot beans gratis, the firm would go bankrupt and the supply would come to an end, just as if everybody were to make their way through barriers designed to prevent them from entering trains that were full, the trains wouldn't start or would break down. My actions, then, were not such as could be universalised. What is more, it is only because of most people's incorrigible tendency to pay for their Heinz beans and respect the injunctions of railway officials that actions such as mine are rendered profitable.

I know this and admit guilt. I venture to make two points only in its extenuation. First, I don't bait officials for most or even much of my time. Most of my actions have always been as universalisable as anybody else's, and I can now scarcely be said to bait officials at all.

Secondly, as I have remarked elsewhere,[1] official baiting contains its element of risk. It requires alertness of body and mind, knowledge of the ways of officials, promptitude in action to forestall them and good nerves. Official-baiting, in fact, keeps you screwed up to concert pitch. (I put it no higher than that, not wishing to invoke the categories of morality by the use of the word "courage"—though, indeed, I might well have done so.)

The Brains Trust

Thirdly, I have been unduly provoked by officials who suspect and dislike me at sight. They seem to have a nose for people like myself which smells us out, distrusts us at smell and induces its owner to neglect, slight and humiliate us whenever he can, even if we have done nothing to deserve

1. See Chapter 1, page 16.

it. When he has to acknowledge our existence, he does so because he can't help it and tries as soon as he possibly can to be rid of the odious necessity for acknowledgment.

Take the Brains Trust for instance. This celebrated institution rose to favour and staked out a claim upon the public ear, when the B.B.C. officials were looking the other way. Devised and staged by a newcomer, Howard Thomas, it began in such a hole and corner way, at a time so obscure, on a programme so dim, that for some time the pundits of the B.B.C. remained largely unaware of its existence. When its growing popularity forced it upon their notice, they were embarrassed and did not know what to do with it. It continued to embarrass them. For one thing, the programme didn't fit in anywhere. It had begun life as "variety", yet "variety" it could scarcely remain. The "Talks Dept." had not thought of it, and from first to last suspected it and were jealous of it ; so it was not "Talks". For some years, I believe, it was specially administered as an anomaly by the "high-ups". It was also an embarrassment that three men should achieve such unpremeditated fame as Huxley, Campbell and myself. The story of how the B.B.C. dealt with the situation, first by reducing our fees and then disbanding us while still at the peak of our popularity, does not belong here. I mention the matter only because it illustrates the way in which, whenever success has come my way, it has been achieved in spite of officials who, on the whole, have disapproved of it, sought to mitigate it while it persisted and to terminate it as soon as they conveniently could.

Especially if they be women. Mercifully, I have known few women in authority, but whenever I have come under the control of one of them, she has made me suffer for it. How scandalously unfair women in authority are. With what ingenuity they excuse themselves for their lack of charity and understanding by invoking the letter of the law ; what a horrid skill they show in outdoing even male officials in discouraging you, putting you off, saying "No" and refusing to give reasons.

For many years as a young man I was an adult education

tutor taking tutorial classes in the evenings, hoping thereby eventually to establish such a connection that I could quit the Civil Service. The peak of the adult education year is the summer school. The tutor goes there for a fortnight or three weeks, takes classes in the morning, plays games in the afternoon and enjoys, if he is so minded, a social evening. He has a holiday and makes a little money. I have enjoyed these schools, which are usually held in pleasant country surroundings, more than any holidays I have had. One's summer school day is composed of just the right amount of work and play, of solitude and society. Indeed, life at these schools conforms with an exactitude which in this imperfect world is as much as one has a right to expect to my recipe for a rightly-lived day.

Trouble at Summer Schools

In the middle of my summer school career a woman—I will be charitable and let her go nameless—a woman, I say, came to the head of things as organising tutor. One summer school I attended under her rule and then down came the ban. I was forbidden to attend any more. That was well over twenty years ago and I have been shut out of these delectable paradises ever since.

Why was the ban imposed? Honestly, I don't know. No doubt I had done a number of potentially "bannable" things. But then, when had I not? Immorality? Well, I might have kissed a girl or two to keep my hand in ; but it was generally taken for granted at that time that I kissed girls at summer schools. Certainly, there was no special disclosure, nothing, I swear, in the way of a scandal.

Ganging and cliquing? Yes, very bad. About a dozen of us formed a gang, sat together at meals, went walks together, hired the tennis court together, played games together in the evening, were visibly full of mutual admiration and audibly full of "gang" jokes. The others must have found us intolerable, especially as our numbers included the prettiest, the best at games, the most intelligent and the most generally attractive and desirable members of the community. But then, ganging and cliquing and being visibly suffused by a feeling of sublime superiority is one of the distinctive pleasures of the visitor to a summer school and, though reprehensible, is not exactly "bannable." Besides, another tutor formed one of the gang and was he banned? He was not.

Irreverence towards and disrespect of authority? Yes, I am afraid, a little. I took part in a somewhat blasphemous revue in which one of us, made up as the woman director, appeared in the role of the Virgin Mary and another, giving a lifelike representation of the administrative organiser, took the part of God. Songs specially written for the occasion were in appropriate vein. Moreover, under the leadership of a profoundly dignified looking individual with an episcopal manner, we used to while away the protracted meal times by loudly chanting hymns and psalms, while our leader would punctuate the courses with loudly intoned responses. This, no doubt, was going far, but it warmed me with the peculiar, private and personal pleasure that disrespect for authority never fails to engender, and I could hardly be expected to forgo so unfailing a pleasure of the self. No doubt, being a tutor and in some sense in authority myself, I should have sought to contribute to and not undermine the respect in which authority was held. Reprehensible? Perhaps. Bannable? I hardly think so.

What the reason for the ban may have been I was never told. I went deviously to work in the hope of finding out but to no purpose. I even tackled the banning woman face to face, asking her point blank why I wasn't invited any more to summer schools. She declined to tell me. When did a woman in authority ever make a concession or show a spark of human feeling to anyone?

I am aware that the foregoing must make me seem such a detestable nuisance that anybody would feel justified in banning me from anywhere. Let me, then, add in the interests of justice that I was a first rate tutor and that students competed fiercely to be allowed to come to my classes.

Importance and Pervasiveness of Officials

The importance of being disliked by officials has grown with the increase in their numbers. That our lives are regulated to an unprecedented degree by a proliferating herd of officials is a commonplace. Officials insert themselves and their forms into every nook and cranny of our existence. Even our homes are no longer inviolate. I forget how many thousands have the right to enter my house—the number, I know, runs into more than a hundred thousand—and at any moment one of them may appear to see if I have a dog or a gun. The garden, perhaps, is our last refuge, the only place yet remaining to us that is reasonably safe from official inspection and infection. And the privacy even of gardens is not for long. Even the garden is threatened by the helicopter.

As their numbers grow, the character of officials changes. Think for a moment of those innumerable young men and women who since the war have entered the administrative grades of the Civil Service. They have taken no grilling examination as we had to do ; they have passed no stringent intellectual test ; but they have been to a house party where they have been vetted by psychologists. Their hair is well-brushed ; they wear their clothes with an air ; they have pleasant manners and agreeable voices and they know to a nicety how to strike the correct mean between deference and familiarity. Cleanly and English-looking, they please the psychologists who report that they have the right complexes or none at all, especially the women psychologists who unfailingly receive the answers they expect. What more can a woman examiner desire ?

Who would not appoint such men? There, at any rate, they are, lurking in their dozens in the bowels of the Foreign Office, the British Council and the B.B.C., looking down their disapproving noses at people like me and saying "No" whenever they get the chance.

All my life I seem to have been thwarted and denied by somebody whom I have never seen but who has, I have no doubt, a nice manner and a genteel mind and a faculty of saying "No."

Scandalous Charge of Lack of Patriotism

There was a time just after the war when the British Council approved of me and sent me abroad to lecture for them, and a very pleasant time I had of it, first in Sweden and then in Belgium, where I was kissed publicly on both cheeks and presented with a medal. Presently a tour was arranged for me in France. I was to visit a number of French Universities, lecturing, so far as I remember, on the future of civilisation—or, it may have been, on English philosophy since the war. I was looking forward very much to this tour. I admire the French above all other peoples, and my gastronomic defences, never strong, go down help-lessly before their wonderful food and drink which is nowhere more elaborately prepared and more gloriously served than on academic occasions, a fact for which I can vouch, having been present at some Descartes celebrations just before the war and been dined and wined to such purpose that I had to retire from the gastronomic field long before the celebra-tions had run their course. Our projected tour was, I remember, to have included Dijon and Toulouse, and we were to motor agreeably and at leisure from place to place. Suddenly the tour was cancelled ; a change of policy, I was told, necessitated by economies ordered from above ! This seemed plausible enough—the Council's budget had recently been curtailed—and for a time I believed it. It was only some years afterwards that I was told that a young man in the Foreign Office had said "No." The reason ? I was believed in some lecture somewhere to have said something unpatriotic.

For once, I was infuriated. I, who love England above all countries, love it to such purpose that I can't bear to be out of it for more than a fortnight at a time, so that again and again, having gone abroad for a holiday, I have come scuttling home before half of it was done in a frenzy of nostalgia ; who love English people whom I think the nicest in the world and am so proud of the English countryside that I judge all others by the standard of the degree of their approximation to the green fields, gentle contours, soft airs and cloudy skies of the land that I know so well—I un-patriotic ? Heavens above !

I may, of course, occasionally have let drop in public a few non-Confucian utterances, but who that is worth his intellectual salt has not ? I do not doubt, again, that I have not always confined my remarks to the platitudes that please officials, being such as they are accustomed themselves to deliver. But I am not after all a diplomatist, and it is only officials who can be trusted always to say the things that officials approve of. Besides, nobody goes voluntarily to hear a lecture by an official.

It is natural to my kind to commit verbal improprieties. We shouldn't be what we are, people whose lectures and addresses the public flocks to hear, if we didn't. It is furthermore natural for any vigorous intellectual thinker, especially if he be of the Left, to traduce existing institutions and to outrage conventional sentiments—the institution of Empire and the sentiment of nationalism, which he takes, as it were, in the stride of his general denunciation among the rest.

The Cases of Shaw and Russell

The interesting thing is that if he goes on doing it long enough, the officials swallow him in the end and pat him and themselves on the back because they have done so. Listen, for example, to Shaw—Shaw, who thirty-five years ago was cut by his friends in the street, asked to resign from his clubs, vilified by the gutter Press, denounced as a traitor and soundly rated for lack of patriotism in the more responsible organs of public opinion, merely because in his pamphlet *Common Sense About the War* (the first world war), he said that if England had taken care to make it plain in advance that she would go to war if Germany marched, there would have been no war, and that the best recipe for preventing war in the future was an alliance between England, France and Germany to ensure the peace of the world—listen, I say, to Shaw : "One can see . . . that our present system of imperial aggression, in which, under pretext of exploration and colonisation, the flag follows the filibuster and trade follows the flag, with the missionary bringing up the rear. . . . " Scarcely the utterance of a patriotic Empire-builder ! Or, an utterance in a different vein : "The imagination cannot conceive a viler criminal than he who should build another London like the present one, nor a greater benefactor than he who should destroy it." Scarcely calculated to conduce to the credit of the capital of the Empire, to inflate national pride in its ownership or to attract foreigners. Yet Shaw, having passed from revolutionary Socialism through general scallywaggery to respectability, finally proceeded from respectability through national figurehead-dom to sainthood. The British Council would have given its very eyes to be able to engage *him* to lecture to the French or to anyone else.

Or take the even more instructive case of Lord Russell. As Bertrand Russell, he was denounced during the 1914-18 war as one of the wickedest men in the country. "Mr. Russell has written a thoroughly mischievous book," wrote Lord Cromer in *The Spectator* in a review of *Principles of Social Reconstruction*, undoubtedly the greatest of Russell's extra-philosophical works. Russell was deprived of his Lectureship at Trinity, his goods and chattels were sold by public auction and I myself remember hearing him denounced and reviled by a Public Prosecutor, shameless under the name of Bodkin—I recall that among his other shortcomings he was charged with the somewhat unexpected sins of irrelevance and the commission of *non sequiturs*—preparatory to being sent to prison for utterances prejudicial to the safety of the State—all this because he ventured to throw doubt upon the prevalent view that the training of young men to acquire skill in slaughter so that they might be willing to kill and capable of killing other young men whenever the State to which they belonged deemed the mass slaughter of the citizens of some other State to be desirable, is the highest duty of the good citizen.

Meanwhile, like all great men, Russell was having his ups and downs with women. Presently he began to publish

41

shocking books. What, for example, could be more out-rageous than the sentiments of *Marriage and Morals*—"Am I to understand, then, that you believe in free love, Mr. Russell ? "—sentiments to which the wickedest school in the country was presently founded to give practical effect. What were those poor children not being taught ?—atheism and anarchism and disrespect for all established institutions certainly ; free love, probably, and things worse, perhaps, than free love, perhaps even homosexuality ! What filthy things people did say about him.

Now there is no doubt that some of his utterances scarcely conformed to the standards of what an official would regard as discreet : "In England men were sent to prison in recent years for expressing disagreement with the Christian religion, or agreement with the teaching of Christ."

Is that the kind of thing which is likely to redound to our credit with foreigners ? "We have prided ourselves upon our territory and our wealth ; we have been ready at all times to defend by force of arms what we have conquered in India and Africa. If we had realised the futility of empire . . ." Are utterances of this kind calculated to increase our prestige abroad ? "The power of the State is a wholly evil thing, quite as evil as the power of the Church which in former days put men to death for unorthodox thought." Is this likely to promote belief in the virtue of the State in general, of the British State in particular and of the swarming officials who are its props, its mirrors and its mouthpieces ?

Yet today Lord Russell has become the recognised spokes-man of the mind and thought of Britain, the official exponent of British culture, the ambassador of the British way of life and thought to the unenlightened foreigner, the darling of the B.B.C., the unfailing stand-by of the British Council, the recipient of honours, the nationally respected sage. (Admittedly he has made things easier for the officials by adjusting some of his utterances to his national position. For example, he has begun to discover virtues in war.)

These late official whitewashings of ex-scallywags give me hope. Perhaps, I think, if I could only continue to keep my end up long enough, perhaps sometime in the eighties even I . . . Who knows ?

Pending, however, my own senile apotheosis, I have to make shift with the pleasures of official baiting. Let me not be misunderstood. I don't bait for choice ; indeed, I would much sooner not bait. But the brutes don't give me any choice. Either they won't leave me alone, or they leave me too severely and pointedly alone in situations and on occasions in which they ought, they really ought, to notice me if they were to pay due and just regard to deserts, ability or even to mere seniority. And so I have to derive such recompense as I can from the pleasures of baiting. Nor, I venture to repeat, are they wholly ignoble pleasures. For the officials hold all the cards. They have so much power, I so little. They, with no trouble at all, can inflict upon me irreparable damage. I can at most cause them a moment's irritation. They are many and I but one. Moreover, they are not embarrassed by the vagaries of the creative temperament. They produce nothing, they create nothing, they contribute nothing. They merely sit and lurk, squashing, castrating and curtailing the productions of others. Or they pass them, having first vetted them and bestowed upon them the seal of their respectable approval. For officials today control all the major avenues of publicity. Think for a moment of the B.B.C. and the use to which it puts its monopoly. "Free speech" say the officials, priding and pluming themselves on their tolerance and protesting the enlightened Liberalism of their views. Yet who, over the air, is allowed to advocate Communism or free love, to press for the mitigation of the laws penalising abortion and homosexuality, to extol the merits of anarchism or polygamy, or to criticise the Roman Catholic Church ? Such protestations are enough to make John Stuart Mill turn in his grave.

Forms of Official Baiting

1. *Ascents of Snowdon.* What forms does official baiting

assume ? Here I come to the tragedy of this chapter, for the question is—it is obvious—one that cannot be answered in public. For to describe the methods by which officials are by me baited, albeit as the years pass with diminishing frequency and success, would be to put them on their guard, as the child playing hide and seek cries out from his hiding place to put the seekers on the scent.

I must, then, content myself with citing one or two cases which are so mellowed by time that they may be said to have entered the category of the early indiscretions of Shaw and Russell. The officials concerned have been dead these many years ; or their teeth have been drawn by retirement. Here, then, are two examples from my early manhood.

In the war of 1914-18 I was a conscientious objector. Tradition, training, conviction and distaste were all bound up in an attitude which seemed so inevitable as to be almost instinctive. War in modern conditions seemed to me the ultimate outrage and anything was preferable to the evils that it entailed and brought in its train. Let those who approved of it fight in it. For myself, I would have no part in it.

I have put the pacifist case often enough in the past and do not here seek either to excuse or defend these convictions. Indeed, it was not until long after the Nazis had appeared, not, in fact, until the summer of 1940 when, with the barbarians at the gates, I sought to join the Home Guard, that it occurred to me that they needed defence. I mention them only to throw into relief my position in the summer of 1916, when, having been granted indefinite leave without pay from the Civil Service, I was wanted by the police for failure to answer my call-up notices. I had been staying for some time at Bryn Corach, Conway, the then headquarters of the Holiday Fellowship whose founder and director, T. H. Leonard, shared my views about the war, extended a kindly, helping hand to conscientious objectors, and rendered in particular the most helpful assistance to their families—for the economic difficulties of men without employment frequently became acute. (So, by the way, did

George Lansbury, the most Christian man I have ever met, who stood a good friend to me at that difficult time).

Leonard gave me little jobs, mainly secretarial, in and about Bryn Corach, which kept me busy, and in return for which I got free board and lodging. One of the highlights of the Bryn Corach week was an expedition to the top of Snowdon. The routine of this expedition was well established and had become almost traditional. The climbing party left Conway early in the morning and took train to Dolwyddelen. From there they climbed Moel Seabod, whence there is a superb view of the Snowdon range, descending about teatime into the valley at Nant Gwynant. After tea the lower slopes of Snowdon were climbed, and between six and seven o'clock the party reached a half-ruined chalet originally built for a mine or quarry manager. The chalet retained its roof, but there were no windows and, apart from a few pots, pans and sacks deposited there by the Holiday Fellowship, the place was without furniture. We made a fire, fetched the water, cooked the food that we had brought, stuffed the sacks with straw to serve as mattresses, and sat round the fire until bed time, telling stories and singing songs. For most of us this was a memorable experience, one that I, at least, have never forgotten. On the following morning we got up early, climbed Snowdon by the Watkin path, came down to Lake Lydau, and then did a prodigious walk either to Bettwys or past Lake Crafnant to Llanrwst and Trefriw, whence we took the train back to Conway.

One day the regular leader of these expeditions fell ill and, as I had already done the journey twice, Leonard asked me if I would like to lead the party in his place. I jumped at the chance. A few days after that an official, whether military, police or merely employment exchange, I cannot now remember, called at Bryn Corach relative to my call-up notice. I, mercifully, was out at the time. It was then that Leonard had his idea. "Why not", he said, "install yourself here as a permanent guide up Snowdon? You can take parties up three times a week, and at any rate

for three nights in every week you will have no address."
I agreed, and for the whole of that summer succeeded in
evading the clutches of the military. At the end of that time
the department to which I belonged, being now desperately
short of staff, recalled me to act as secretary to a Government Committee, and thereafter I was too overworked to
have time to think about the Army or even the war.

Now to say that I enjoyed my ascents of Snowdon very
much indeed, that I enjoyed leading the party, enjoyed being
in charge of domestic operations, selecting this one to make
the fire, that one to do the cooking and those the washing
up, that I enjoyed seeing dim, closed personalities opening
out and blossoming under the stimulus of the strange conditions, that I enjoyed above all a loving pride in knowing
every step of the *route* so that by the end of the summer I
became a minor expert on one face of Snowdon—to say this
and much more in the same vein, though true, would be
nothing to the purpose of this chapter. For added to these
sources of enjoyment was another, a more individual pleasure
—that of evading and bamboozling the officials whom I
liked to picture looking for me. This was a pleasure all my
own, a private pleasure, a personal pleasure, a pleasure of
the self.

2. *Coats and Hats.* When the war was over, I fell into the
doldrums. I don't suppose that God ever intended me to be
a Civil Servant—for one thing I was too badly dressed and
slovenly—but I had bad luck and was not too well treated.
In a word I was shelved, and with little work and no chance
of promotion dragged out eleven weary years from 1919 to
1930, when I secured a merciful discharge complete with a
small pension. During the whole of that miserable period
my hopes and thoughts were centred on one thing—how to
get out. I had a wife and children to support, and had
to be assured of a certain income. It is difficult for any
but the most eminent Civil Servant to secure a job outside
the Service. Moreover, as I have already mentioned,
nobody has ever evinced much disposition to appoint me
to anything. My hope was that by writing books and articles

and taking classes in the evening, I might ultimately become sufficiently well-known to obtain a University post or at least to make a living by authorship, journalism and tutoring. So I took my diminishing Civil Service work with diminishing seriousness and spent an increasing amount of the time which should have gone to the dictating of letters, the inditing of minutes and the composing of memoranda, to preparing lectures and writing books. I had first call upon the services of a typist—a hangover, this, from the days when I had been overworked—and she, bless her, used to type books and articles for me in Civil Service time on Civil Service paper. Thus I obtained gratis at Government expense, pens, nibs, ink, a desk, a typist and a typewriter, enjoying the while a salary which, though very far from being handsome, was at least secure. Many would-be authors would have envied me my chains. Only in one respect did they gall ; I had to be there ; I had to keep office hours. So long as I shared a room with two other men this necessity was very disabling, since they could not but know whether I was in the office or not. Moreover, under their vigilant eyes I could not busy myself as I wished to do with my own work. I could not, for example, read books. For some years I chafed badly under these restrictions, and was very miserable indeed. I did the best I could for myself; I built up and habitually retained great piles of Government files as a screen and read philosophy under their cover, but the device was far from satisfactory. I was always being interrupted or made to gossip, and at any moment some fool might come and look over my shoulder. So I absented myself for long periods in the lavatory where I could read without interruption. I read, I remember, the whole of *A Midsummer Night's Dream* sitting on the lavatory seat—not, however, at one sitting.

It was only when I obtained a room of my own that I was in a position to devise the coat and hat system. My department, the Ministry of Labour, a very large one, was at that time housed partly in Montagu House, now pulled down, and partly in a scatter of bungalows that had proliferated

from the back of Montagu House in both directions along
the Embankment. Civil Service work unavoidably involves
a certain amount of absence from one's room at conferences
and committees and for the purpose of conferring with
other officials, and in that vast sprawling building, to find
a man who was temporarily out of his room might take a
considerable time. He might be anywhere in the building,
though, as long as he *was* in it, his hat and overcoat—all
officials wore overcoats ; some also donned special office
jackets and discarded their everyday coats, which they
hung upon pegs—would be visible in his room, witnesses
to his presence in the office. It was of these facts that my
system proposed to take advantage.

In its first inception it amounted to little more than
leaving a hat and coat hanging on the peg, when I was out
of the office. But in its maturity it was a much more elaborate affair. My room contained a fair-sized cupboard of
which I possessed a key. In this I used to keep a varied
assortment of hats, never less than three, and a number of
coats varying from alpaca through light summer to a heavy
winter overcoat. There were also two mackintoshes and a
couple of scarves. Upon this assortment of garments I used
to ring the changes, placing them in prominent positions in
the room, albeit with a studied carelessness as if they had
been hurriedly hung or thrown down, as visible witnesses of
my presence in the office. It was, I thought, important to
avoid anything stereotyped, anything which would look
like a rigging of the room with stage properties by an
occupant who wished to disguise his absence. So the caller
would find a hat hanging on a peg or dropped on the desk or
on the seat of a chair. Over the back of the chair an overcoat or mackintosh would be flung. A scarf obviously
dropped hurriedly by somebody too preoccupied to
concern himself with the correct disposal of his discarded
garments, would be thrown over a side table, or would
droop negligently over one corner of the desk.

There was no end to the permutations and combinations
of garments and of the placing of garments that I devised for

throwing dust into the eyes of those of my chiefs and sub-ordinates who might be curious as to my whereabouts. Under cover of these arrangements I kept disgraceful hours. I would arrive at 10.30, give evidence of my presence by going to see one or two people and depart for lunch about twelve ; I would stay out till three or four o'clock in the afternoon, when I would hurry back to see if I had been wanted during my absence. Presently I began to omit the hurrying back and would take the afternoon off to play tennis. On such afternoons it was my hope and intention not to have to return at all, but I would take the precaution of making a telephone call on some official matter to a relevant colleague in order to remind him of my existence. He was not, after all, to know that the call came from the changing room of my tennis club.

At the end I was spending no more than a couple of hours a day at the office, this minimum attendance being still rendered necessary by my dependence on the typist so considerately provided by the department—I couldn't, you see, get *her* out of the office since she shared a room with a number of others. That my conduct was reprehensible I allow ; but I had my excuses. At one time I had worked hard in the Civil Service and striven to make a career there for myself. I had not been well paid but had comforted myself with the thought of the promotion which would one day be mine. I didn't like the obscurity, but looked forward to the Civil Servant's reward, the exercise of power.

I was not promoted, but regularly passed over. More-over, as I have told, I was given less and less work to do. Yet I was neither stupid nor unwilling, and many men no better adapted than myself to official life had done reason-ably well in the Civil Service. It was, I am afraid, the same old story that I have had and shall have occasion to tell so often in this book. The eminent and authoritative persons who controlled my destinies either disliked or distrusted me or both. I was not safe and reliable ; I was not sufficiently responsible ; above all, I was not discreet. What resource, then, was left to me save that of quitting the Service as soon as I could, making meanwhile the most of such opportunities of official-baiting as I could contrive? Thus the hats and coats served a double purpose, killing, as it were, two birds with a single stone. First, they paved the way for my eventual exit from the place of my confinement and discomfiture. Secondly, they enabled me to enjoy the pleasure of scoring off officialdom, scoring with a purely private and personal pleasure, a pleasure of the self.

3. *Scoring off the War.* It is my consciousness of the somewhat unfavourable light in which these episodes may have placed me, rather than the recognition of any very obvious common thread running through the experiences just described and my Birkbeck war-time lectures, that emboldens me to conclude with a brief allusion to a slightly more creditable incident in my career. Yet the thread is there in the common character of the enjoyments derived. For, in the case of the Birkbeck lectures, too, I was scoring off authority, albeit the authority in this case was feared and thwarted not by me alone, but by the rest of my fellow countrymen, so that, in enjoying the pleasures of "official baiting", I was for once on the popular side, which was also, at any rate for the time, the safe side.

When the war of 1939-1945 began, all the Colleges of the University of London were evacuated save one. This College, my own, remained behind, since the great majority of its students were engaged in earning their living during the day time and could not, therefore, leave London. It had been intended that the College should close, but after the first few dazed weeks it took courage and resumed its evening courses. All those who were connected with the place, not least myself, were profoundly grateful to the courage and vision displayed by the authorities responsible for this decision. Throughout the war we were all of us very glad of Birkbeck, but particularly during those first weeks which were accompanied by an almost complete cultural blackout. Theatres closed, pictures were sent away, meetings called off, concerts cancelled. Each day brought the news of some fresh closure or cancellation.

When the National Gallery lunch-hour concerts started, they were like a light burning in the darkness. Starved of beauty, people rushed to hear them and the salon in which they were held was crowded. People enjoyed feeling not only that civilisation was somehow "carrying on," but that they were helping to carry it.

The success of the concerts gave us an idea. If people would go to hear music in the lunch-hour, why not lectures ? There would not be so many, of course ; there might not even be enough to justify the lectures ; but the experiment was worth trying and we tried it accordingly. And so, just when the blackout was beginning to close down on us, the enterprising authorities of my College arranged for me to give a series of lunch-hour lectures lasting from 1.15 to 2. I lectured on such subjects as *Leading Ideas of Greek Philosophy*, *Plato's Republic* and *Aristotle's Ethics*. The attendances were large from the first, and presently, as the Brains Trust brought my name before the public, they became very large. The lectures were given in circumstances of some hardship. The College theatre, the only available lecture room of the requisite size, was bombed early in the war and the heating system was put out of action. It was bitterly cold ; presently holes and gaps appeared in the roof, and the rain came through. On one occasion I lectured in a heavy overcoat with snowflakes falling through the dim purlieus of the theatre. The College technicians endeavoured to counter these difficulties by electric fires, their most ingenious device being the insertion of a small fire in the hollow of the reading desk on which I rested my notes. One day the desk began to smoke. The audience tittered with amusement. Suddenly a lady in the front row gave a little scream. The desk had burst into flames. The electricity had been too much for it.

The audience on the whole rejoiced in its hardships. There is something to be said for the view that people, at any rate in England, only value "culture" if it is made difficult of access. One thinks of poor boys reading in ice-cold garrets by the light of a guttering candle ; of miners

51

rushing from the pit-head to change their clothes and get a bite of bread and cheese before cycling four or five miles to the nearest W.E.A. class. These are the salt of the educational earth and the books they read, the essays they write, the ideas to which they are introduced make upon their intellectual consciousness an impression which is all the sharper by reason of the sacrifice of leisure and comfort which they have made to get their "book learning". How retentively one's own memory holds the list of historical dates or the lines of repetition which one got up early in the morning to learn, or the "sticky" bit of Thucydides which one "prepared" as one sat up late at night when the rest of the world had gone to bed.

I have lectured to no keener audiences than those which sat in the cracking cold of the College theatre, nibbling their sandwiches while the snowflakes fell through the roof and the desk crackled in flames on the platform.

After the lecture we had a lunch. These jovial occasions were made a shade gayer and heartier than they otherwise would have been—and, given the company, they would always have been enjoyable enough—by our knowledge that we had somehow "pulled a fast one" over the war. We all, I think, felt this in our degree. We were first and foremost teachers and educationists. Our natural traffic was in ideas, and the war had blacked out all the things which gave our lives meaning. So far as London was concerned, the commerce of ideas unconnected with the war had practically ceased. Nowhere else, so far as we knew, was any adult person receiving education in subjects unconnected with the acquisition of skill in the slaughter of his fellow men. Behind the war stood Hitler and the Nazis. We knew that if they won, the free life of the mind, as we understood it, would cease, cease for as long as their *régime* stood, and that civilisation would enter a new dark age. So it seemed to us then ; so it still seems to me now. Thus in trying to beat the Nazis we were fighting for the maintenance of the conditions in which civilisation, as we understood it, could continue. And here, in the very process of

52

fighting for it, we were contriving to enjoy a little of that for which we fought. It was like picking strawberries for market and eating one or two while you picked, or having a taste of the Christmas pudding while it was in the stirring, than which, as everybody agrees, nothing could be nicer.

Now I am aware that this incident of the Birkbeck lectures and all that is connected with it may not seem at first sight to belong to the same category as those hitherto mentioned. It doesn't on the surface look like official-baiting. The reason for the apparent dissimilarity is that on this occasion the officials and colleagues of my College were on my side— and so, no doubt, for once, are my readers—which is doubtless why during those early years of the war I was sensible of a profound contentment. For once I was with and not at loggerheads with my fellows. My hopes and wishes were theirs ; my hand was not against them, nor theirs against me. For we were all together engaged in baiting that vastest and most monstrous of all officials—the God of War.

I hope it will not set the reader too much against me, if I avow that the pleasure I experienced in giving those early wartime lectures in the face of every discouragement of material circumstance bore, in spite of its outward seeming reputability, a family resemblance to those other pleasures of which you have read in this chapter with such censorious disapproval.

CHAPTER IV

The Pleasures of Not Taking a Sunday Walk

> "A respectable family taking a walk
> Is a subject on which I could dwell.
> It contains all the virtues that ever there were
> And points us a moral as well,"

or words to that effect. (I have lost, alas, the book of Belloc's—Heartless Rhymes I think it was called—in which this admirable verse appeared.)

One sees them in their dozens on a Sunday on Hampstead Heath, these respectable families taking their walk, the mother, the baby in its pram, the little boy or the little girl and the father. What of the father? He is usually bored and miserable even when he doesn't know it. He is not talking to his wife. How could he be, since they have met every day and all night of the week, and every week of the year, since, being a respectable family, they take their holidays together—and he has long ago exhausted whatever in the way of contents her mind may once have possessed.

Courtship

In their early days, when he was trying to win her, he indulged, no doubt, in the display common to most males at courtship times. And since he is an urban Englishman, his display may well have included a few intellectual tricks. He may have known something of politics and discoursed to her on Socialism or of the wickedness of Communists or Tories. Or he may have had ideals, vegetarian, perhaps, or pacifist, and sought to induce her to feed with him on nuts and hay or to attend meetings of the Peace

Pledge Union, as he dilated on his personal stand against war and conscription. Or he may have been a chess player or a hobby hunter or a collector. . . . Whatever his interest may have been, he talked to her eagerly and abundantly, telling her his plans and ambitions, expounding to her the niceties of his subject and displaying his mastery of them, and as he discoursed earnestly, vividly and, perhaps, humorously, gesticulating the while, he made her realise what a fine fellow he was, and since he was himself passionately interested and wished her to share his interests he was, no doubt, for the nonce, interesting. And she?—she, too, felt an interest in what he was saying and responded after her manner. For the Life Force, or what used to be called Mother Nature, or whatever it is that brings human beings together to serve a purpose that transcends them by continuing the species, taking no account of community of interests, of similarity of outlook or of temperamental affinities, provided only that the purpose be served, endows women at such times with a great power of receptiveness and intellectual sympathy. It is not merely that they *appear* to wish to share the tastes, to understand the discussions and to abet the ambitions ; they do in truth wish to share, to understand and to abet. And for the time their wish is granted, so that they contrive some measure of understanding of "the subject", interest themselves in the creed or the cause and sympathise with the ambitions, with the result that much talk of a bright, helpful and elevating kind goes on between them. So fowlers cover twigs with lime to snare the birds and entomologists sugar trees with molasses to attract the moths.

Marriage

But all that is long past and done with.   It has served its purpose and the bird is in the net.   And now, the ideals forgotten and the ambitions faded, the poor chap has subsided from his earth-shaking *rôle* of revolutionary leader, Prime Minister, Napoleon of business, great painter or chess master into that of breadwinner for wife and children.

And so there is nothing to talk about as they go for their respectable walk. Nor is there anybody else to talk to, for the family speaks to nobody ; it keeps itself scrupulously to itself, its only concern with the rest of the world being that it should put up as good a show as possible before the neighbours.

The walk is very lackadaisical. Perhaps the husband is throwing a ball for the little boy or a stick for the dog or he is just respectably pushing the pram. If it is summer he is eating his sandwiches lounging on the grass, where, respectable as they are, the family takes care to leave its litter behind it. I am overcome with compassion for this man in whom the lamp of life burns so dimly.

Why is it that these eminently respectable couples, these good citizens who act as they ought and give the community the answers that it expects, who live in so secure a dullness, fill me with melancholy ? It is because they stand in my mind for waste of talent, for slackness, inertia and apathy, for lack of enterprise, initiative and adventure; because in them or, rather, in him, the lamp does indeed burn dimly. Nothing that he is saying or doing requires effort or skill ; there is nothing in his environment to stimulate him to performance or display. His talents are unused ; his energies lie dormant ; he is living at half-cock.

I don't deny the importance of these people ; they are the healthy cells of the body politic. They are like a quiet river moving easily and uneventfully through placid pastures to the sea. They are the citizens who make the wheels of the community go round and do their duty in that state of life to which they have been called. They are, no doubt, the salt of the earth. But their happiness, if happy they are, frightens and slightly disgusts me. The happiness is enjoyed on too easy terms. It is the happiness of the vegetable, and acquiescence in the limitations of the life that offers it argues something of the vegetable in the nature of those who acquiesce. Hence, to me, the Sunday walkers are a distressing sight. Never do I cease to thank God that I am not like unto them.

For I have sought—or so I like to think—to purchase happiness on harder terms.[1] I have wanted my life to be like a rushing stream whose course was beset by rocks, even if on occasion its impetuosity took me on to them. (I did not know, when I formed this ideal, how heavy is the price which society exacts from those who leave the green pastures which it has laid out for them.) And so, contemplating the Sunday walkers, I have rarely failed to say, "There, but for the grace of God, go I."

Women and the Sunday Walk

For I so nearly did. Or rather, I had to make such frantic efforts, hurting myself and other people so much in the process, in order to avoid doing so. All the women into whose hands I have been at different times committed have tried to turn me into a respectable Sunday walker—all except one and she, poor dear, died before the claims of respectability had begun seriously to exert themselves. (Besides, her period was the early 'twenties and her territory, which was also mine, Chelsea, a time and a place as remote from Sunday pram-pushing as could well be imagined. Being in full revolt from the well-to-do-military household and the upstanding girls' school in which she had been brought up, she saw herself as a writer and/or painter, and desired neither children nor respectability. She was ferociously independent. A fierce independence was our outstanding characteristic in those Chelsea days. Even when we went to parties—and we went to a great many— we took our own bottles of drink with us. That was a care-free age, a little space of gaiety and light-heartedness vouchsafed to us between the horror of the first world war and the gathering gloom of the 'thirties. We all seemed to be of much the same age, and there was a good deal of what used to be called "sleeping around".)

From the others I escaped before, by producing children and so acquiring dependence, they had me clamped down beyond the possibility of escape. The great thing, I found,

---

1. See the Chapter on The Pleasures of Hurdles.

was to live with women who were sufficiently attractive to have a reasonable prospect of being taken over by somebody else when our connection reached its appointed end. This involved misery of the most extreme when, in spite of my impassioned protestations and threats of suicide, the still attractive woman left me for another, but at least it did ensure freedom from the burden of the economic upkeep of a woman one no longer cared for.

Incident of the Treacle

Not but what I have begotten children in my time, in point of fact, three, all of them, God be praised, born in legitimate wedlock, who for a time did, indeed, bid fair to weave me into the pattern of respectable family life. What saved me—at least, so far as the Sunday walk was concerned—was the incident of Aggie and the treacle. Aggie was my first child and must, I suppose, at the time of the incident have been about a year old. We lived in a cottage in the village of West Humble which lies at the foot of Box Hill, near the Burford Bridge Hotel. At the time of which I am writing, some thirty-five years ago, this beautiful part of Surrey had still to feel the impact of progress. There was no by-pass road lying like a weal left by the whiplash of civilisation upon the fair face of the land, along which a torrent of cars rushed destructively to the coast, and the Burford Bridge Hotel was itself still the country inn about which Stevenson had written. Behind it lay the great house in which Sir William Durning Lawrence, Bart., meditated upon the authorship of the plays of Shakespeare. As yet few family parties had found their way up the slopes of Box Hill to leave their Sunday visiting cards in the shape of litter scattered over its green flanks.

It was on a pious undergraduate pilgrimage to Meredith who lived at Flint Cottage at the bottom of one of the valleys that cut into the folds of the hill, that I had first seen and fallen in love with this tract of country. And when my wife, knowing that her baby was on its way, pleaded to have it out of London—she hated the war and even in 1916 was afraid of bombs—it seemed natural to go to Box Hill. Here we were installed in a picturesque but insanitary cottage, whence I travelled daily up to Whitehall. We were too poor to afford a nurse, and were looked after by the owner of the cottage, a bullying, hard-faced woman with a wall eye. On Sundays we used to go out for the day taking our lunch, a respectable family taking its respectable walk, with myself for the first and only time in my life pushing the pram containing Aggie, spare napkins, and the lunch. On the day of the incident the luncheon provisions included a large, freshly opened tin of Lyle's golden syrup. For a time all went well. Presently, however, we left the road and took a footpath through the fields, a footpath which in due course brought us to a stile. My wife proposed to take either the luncheon or the baby or both out of the pram before it was lifted over. I, however, besotted by *hubris*, insisted that I should lift them over together. When the pram, approaching the top of the stile, reached its angle of maximum inclination to the ground, the tin of treacle, insecurely poised, toppled over, the lid fell off, and the contents poured themselves over the baby's head and face. At the first impact of the cool, sticky fluid the baby opened its mouth to howl, whereat a thick stream of treacle poured through the orifice down its throat. The results were terrible ; the pram was in an indescribable mess, knives, forks, plates, bits of food, nappies, clothes and child being stuck together in a single, glutinous mass. The child, suddenly suspended in mid-howl, began to choke, was suspected (wrongly) of breaking a blood-vessel, and hurried, all treacly, to the doctor. It was my wife who later pushed the mournful pram home. For my part I was never allowed to push it again. Thus, though the father of children, I escaped for all time the baser ignominies of the respectable Sunday walk.

Presently we went to live in Hampstead where, indeed, with the exception of two adjournments to Chelsea, I have lived ever since. These last must themselves be regarded in the light of flights from the Sunday walk, since in each case they involved the surrender of an old and respectability-acquiring establishment and the setting up of a new one, complete with a new partner. When the latter in due course felt herself established, she craved for respectability like her predecessors and so, after a brief interlude in Chelsea, I found myself back again in Hampstead. None, however, was successful in her attempts to subdue me to the Sunday walk on the Heath.

The Suburban Tennis Club

My escape lay for many years through tennis. I joined a small and highly respectable suburban club in the Garden Suburb and fairly early on a Sunday morning I would go there on my bicycle, taking lunch. About half past twelve the members of the Club, most of whom lived in the block of flats to which the tennis courts belonged, would disappear for their Sunday dinner. This, taken in the communal dining room, was the highlight of their gastronomic week. Each family sat at its separate little table, addressing from time to time a polite word to its neighbours, but for the most part, like the walkers, keeping itself primly to itself. To one another, husband and wife spoke practically not at all ; some were not on speaking terms, the others had nothing left to say. It was, indeed, a very respectable occasion, and as the luncheon was both abundant and prolonged, it extended itself over a considerable period.

Meanwhile, I was sitting on the tennis court eating my bread, cheese and onion, and drinking my flask of wine. I had not yet brought the business of *al fresco* lunching to the pitch of perfection described elsewhere in this book, and the value of the claret and onions, often Spanish onions, was largely symbolic. What they symbolised was my unfitness for and eventual rejection by the genteel society to whose fringes, through my need of tennis, I precariously clung. (I am not sure, but I seem to remember that my breath was noticed and animadverted upon by some of the lady players, always as sensitive to smells as they are callously insensitive to noise.) When the residents from the flats, bloated with food and inclined to be liverish and cross, returned to the courts for their afternoon game, there was I, larky and spry, in possession of the best court ready to receive them.

I used to stay till about four o'clock, and then went home to tea, the family-walk danger period having been safely surmounted for one more Sunday.

Oh, the pleasures of those vagrant and ill-conditioned Sundays—the pleasure of being out there alone on the court, eating my own food and not in there in the dining room eating the large disabling meal that the Sunday ritual of suburban respectability enjoined ; the pleasure of not being with the family ; of not taking its walk or pushing its pram ; the pleasure, in a word, of being myself and not what society would have me be.

Of course I paid for it, since, as I have already told,[1] society always takes it out of those of its members who don't offer it the behaviour it expects.

However hard I try to serve it according to its lights, it has never once rewarded *me* with an honour. My kind must *take* everything that they can get, not so much because we are naturally predatory as because society never gives anything away—not, at least, to us. And since in respect of nineteen-twentieths of us we are the creatures of that society, shaped by its environment, formed by its training and precepts, nurtured on its education and public opinion and, therefore, in respect of these nineteen-twentieths, exactly like everybody else, wanting what everybody else wants, and desiring to be honoured as others are honoured, I mind all this very much. What is more, as I grow older and the twentieth part, the self native and untamed, the self primitive and proper, is increasingly submerged under the *débris* of social accretion, I mind it more and more. This pleasure of the self that I have described, the pleasure of not taking the Sunday walk, is but a small compensation for the slights administered by society. Still, it exists.

---

1. See The Pleasures of Official Baiting.

CHAPTER V

The Pleasures of Outdoor Food

ONE of the pleasures of *my* self is food. It is a pleasure that grows greater as I grow older. The other pleasures of the body, the pleasures in games, in walking, riding, scrambling over mountains and in making love, fail and fade ; no new pleasure of the mind comes to take their place ; the pleasures of the spirit, whether active as in religious experience or ruminative as in recollection and contemplation, are still dormant. Broadly, only the pleasure of food remains— remains, and as the years pass increases, for although I have no longer my old appetite, I make up for it in greediness. Yet I do not wish to write a chapter on food, not because I have not much to say on this topic but because others have said it and said it often ; some of them, a few, have said it better than I could say it.

On English cooking, for example, I could spread myself over several pages of spleen. Indeed, on this subject I *will* permit myself a word, not merely to indulge myself in the pleasure of hitting back, but because it links on to the two pleasures of the self of which I propose here to write, the pleasure of invention and the pleasure of display.

English Cooking. Why Worse ?

Before the war English cooking was so bad that it was hard to believe that it could deteriorate. That it has done so, plumbing depths of culinary squalor hitherto unknown is, I judge, due to three factors :—

1. The excellence of the materials traditionally available for English cooking and, more particularly, the meat. This was so good that the simplest culinary operation, such as,

roasting or boiling, was sufficient to bring it to a condition of excellence. All that was necessary was to enable it, as it were, to be itself. The fact that in the '30's it rarely was itself, that the traditional dishes of English plain cooking were snares and cheats, that the Aylesbury duck was not Aylesbury, the Surrey fowl not Surrey, the Yorkshire ham not Yorkshire, the Banbury cake not Banbury, that of the lamb and green peas the first came not from the South Downs but from New Zealand, having been frozen and eviscerated of its taste *en route,* and the peas not from the garden but from a tin or from one of those horrible cartons of chopped up gobbets of mixed vegetables called Russian salad, that the ingredients of the traditional plum or raspberry tart were introduced for the first time upon one's plate, the pastry having been bought ready made in little cubes and squares and then warmed up and the plums or raspberries having only just emerged from their tins or jars and been separately warmed up, the whole being served with a dollop of synthetic cream—all these and many other analogous phenomena peculiar to England were testimonies less to any deterioration of the materials of English plain cooking, than to the fact that the English had grown too numerous for the materials, as it were, to go round, and were either compelled to resort to such substitutes as the commerce of the Empire could provide, or were grown too blunted and brutish in respect of their sensibilities to notice that they *were* substitutes, or so corrupted that they had come to prefer them.

2. The unadaptability and lack of inventiveness of English cooking women. Faced during the war by the lack of many of the materials necessary for the traditional English dishes, they did not adapt themselves to changed circumstances by improvising new dishes from the resources available ; they continued to produce the old ones without the materials that had once made them tolerable. Thus they continued to make suet puddings without suet and plum duffs without currants and raisins and to serve stewed fruit without cream. They contrived to make blancmanges which

consisted entirely of cornflour and water, and continued to fry what little meat there was when there was no fat to fry it in.

3. Their laziness and dislike of food. Previously these traits were subject to certain inhibitions. Many women had few ascertainable reasons for existence except the care of houses and the preparation of meals. Some sort of show had, therefore, to be put up. But when the war came, many working class women went into factories and were thus provided with a heaven-sent alibi, while middle-class women living in a world no longer cushioned by working-class maids, were too immersed in the care of their children and the crude labours of the house to have time for the subtleties of the kitchen. Thus a variety of circumstances combined to enable English women to indulge without stint or scruple in their lazy indifference to the arts of the kitchen, and to give free play to their vaunted contempt—"I don't hold with those Frenchified messes ! "—for the pleasures of the palate.

The Sandwich

These conditions still obtain. Nowhere is their incidence more severely felt than in the preparation of meals to be eaten out of doors. A meal to be eaten out of doors means, to the English mind, one thing and one thing only—sandwiches. "Going out for the day, are you," Then you would like some sandwiches to take with you," says the manager of the hotel with a smile on her false, fat face, as if she were bestowing a benediction.

Of the sandwich considered as an article of diet there is one advantage and two disadvantages. The advantage is that it is compact, and that a packet of sandwiches goes economically into the pocket—which, no doubt, is why Lord Sandwich in an ill-advised moment devised it. Of its disadvantages one is inherent in the conception of the sandwich, the other incidental to its preparation by idle, stingy or incompetent women which means, in fact, that it is practically universal. The inherent disadvantage consists in the double as opposed to the single wall of bread, a circumstance which results in the provision of twice as much bread in relation to the allowance of meat as is desirable, customary or is, indeed, eaten in any other connection. The only ways of dealing with this defect are to put two and not one layer of beef, pork, ham or whatever it may be between the bread walls, or to dispense with one of the walls, so that a pile of sandwiches runs bread, meat, followed by bread, meat, and not bread, meat, bread followed by bread, meat, bread. But, this would be to destroy the concept of this comestible ; the thing would be no longer a sandwich.

The defect incidental arises from the concealing character of the walls. Unless one disintegrates the sandwich on its production, one cannot see what the walls contain or conceal. In point of fact, they have usually concealed very little and, in these post-war years, the little has shrunk to an exiguity which increasingly approximates to nothingness. In its pre-war prime the sandwich would contain one slice of ham ; but the ham might consist mostly of fat or of fat and gristle. In a luncheon basket purchased by me at Aberystwyth Railway Station I have discovered a sandwich containing gristle and nothing else—a strictly uneatable comestible. (I kept it for some months as an exhibit, to illustrate my contention that in so far as it is possible to dig beneath the depths, the food and cooking of Wales have always been a degree more debased than the food and cooking of England.) And it was but rarely that the sandwich-preparer thought to add mustard or to butter the bread.

Now the fact that these deficiencies could be concealed from the potential eater by the natural formation of the comestible, enabled the sandwich to become a challenge to the meanness, the indifference or the incapacity of the preparer. And chiefly to the meanness. What a lot of money hotel and farmhouse proprietors must have made out of sandwich lunches !

The food shortages occasioned by the war by making the preparation of a sandwich at once agreeable and sustaining in any event difficult, brought them a golden opportunity, an opportunity which was too good to be missed. And it was not missed. Farmhouses in such areas as, for example, the Lake District, which were known for their provision of a plain but hearty, albeit expensive, dietary, would give their patrons sandwiches containing fish paste or meat paste, or sandwiches impregnated with Bovril or beef essence or smeared with Marmite. Presently these wretched meat substitutes were themselves eroded, and I have taken out for a full day's walking or even climbing, sandwiches containing no more than a smear of some totally unrecognisable synthetic food—a ghost of an essence, a mere fragrance upon the mountain air. It is to be remembered that to this meagre diet nine times out of ten nothing was added ; the tenth time, it would be eked out by one of those inimitable cakes made without fat and containing perhaps two currants but surrounded by a frill, such as are peculiar to and distinctive of England.

As for drink, no spontaneous provision of drink has to my knowledge ever been made, though after a certain amount of pressure I have sometimes managed to secure the addition of a bottle of beer. . . .

Eating Out of Doors in France—

I remember the first packed lunch I was ever given in France. I was staying as a young man in a small hotel in a corner of south-western France, where a little promontory of French territory stretches out to make a dent in the frontier of Spain. The two of us had gone out for the day for a scramble in the foothills of the Pyrenees. The lunch was as follows : First, olives, radishes, some sardines, butter and a long thin loaf. Another loaf had been split down the middle ; most of the "crumb" had been taken out and along the hollow thus left had been stretched a long thin omelette *fines herbes*. There were several slices of veal jellied along the edges, together with a number of slices of a delicious *pâté*. With these there was a green salad packed in a carton through the seams of which a little of the salad dressing had

66

seeped. There were a couple of peaches and some green figs. There were two cream cakes and there was a large slice of Brie cheese. Half a bottle of white wine and half a bottle of red completed this lunch, which was beautifully packed in two small baskets.

Now the memory of this lunch, an extremely good one even by French standards, has, as I said, remained with me and a time came when I began to ask myself whether I could not myself contrive something on the same lines—not, of course, so good as the original model, that I could never have aspired to—but something that was not at least a culinary disgrace, something that a French working-class lad would not have thrown in his mother's face.

—And in England

For many years I had the advantage of a housekeeper who, though English, had some feeling for food. We made a speciality of lunches to be taken for a day's walk and eaten out of doors. Here is a sample :—a French loaf, accompanied by an omelette placed when cold in a long plastic container resembling the containers which people purchase for the accommodation of tooth brushes and toilet requisites. Some slices of meat or the wing of a chicken. Spring onions, a piece of Camembert or Brie and fruit in season. I have a personal *penchant* for slices of plum pudding. I have always held that the kind of plum pudding that one enjoyed as a schoolboy—"spotted dick," or "spotted dog" or "currant roll" or whatever it might be called—embodied a fundamentally sound idea. But these school puddings suffered from a grave defect ; there were never enough currants and raisins embedded in the suet. Enormously increase the proportion of the currants and raisins, add plenty of sugar or honey, steep in rum when cooking, and you have an admirable comestible. Like so many eatables—stews, hot-pots, soups—it gets better with renewed cooking. Prepared at the beginning of the week and heated up thereafter as occasion requires, cut into slices, coated again with sugar, and packed cold in greaseproof paper, this sort of

67

pudding makes an admirable conclusion to an out of door meal. Add a small flask of sherry and half a bottle of red wine—a good Algerian will do—and you have a meal which at least does not disgrace the French model on which it was first conceived.

For more than twenty years I have experimented with different varieties of out-of-door meals. The devising and testing of these meals has been one of the pleasures of the self, one of the few avenues along which my creative spirit has found expression. (But that is to do myself more than justice, for it suggests that a great turbulence of creativity is surging against the doors of inhibition or repression or social convention or whatever it may be by which it is denied an outlet. In fact, my creative spirit is a poor affair and for its feeble and intermittent pulsations I am only too ready to afford whatever channels of expression it will consent to irrigate. But channel away as I may, there is not much of a flow.)

They vary, of course, with the seasons. In winter a properly constructed pork pie whose pastry is so well made and so little obtrusive that you actually find yourself wishing there were more of it—that it should evoke such a wish is, I take it, the greatest excellence of which pastry is capable— or some slices of cold pork may be taken. If the latter they are always accompanied with pickles. If these are onions, they must be properly prepared and pickled, which means that they must be prepared and pickled at home. But there still survive some brands of piccalilli or mustard pickle, which can be eaten without scarifying the skin of one's tongue. The packing of this sort of comestible, which formerly presented a problem, has been solved by the blessed invention of plastic containers of all shapes and sizes, light, water-tight, and easily carried.

The English have known about thermos flasks for years, but never—at least to my knowledge—has it occurred to them to use them for any purpose save the containing of hot milk, tea or coffee. I consider one of the most out- standing tokens of our culinary degeneracy to be the almost total disappearance of hot concoctions from the average repertory of English drinking. Up to and including the time of Dickens, English literature is full of accounts of toddies, neguses and punches, but if you ask for a hot drink in an English pub today, even if it be only the hotting up of rum and whisky, they stare at you with consternation. This man, the pert girl behind the bar obviously supposes, must be mad. But I have sworn to myself not to dilate on the barbarism of English eating and drinking, so will resume my *rôle* of constructive creation.

The hot drink which I favour has a basis of rum and milk which belong to that heaven-sent category of combinations, of which ham and eggs, lamb and mint sauce, duck and green peas, ham and peas, Claret and cold pheasant, oysters and Champagne are prominent examples, sweetened with honey. In order to avoid clotting, the honey must first be melted on the fire in one of those little coffee pots that one buys in Soho and then poured in liquid form into the rum and milk. Lemon may be added and a sprinkling of nutmeg, but not much. The difficulty of this drink is so to prepare it that the milk does not curdle ; the drawback, the absurd expensiveness of that best Empire product—rum. Take this drink hot with you in a thermos, and on a cold winter's day you will have a wonderful pleasure from your lunch in the wood.

So much for the pleasures of invention. Now for the pleasures of display.

Lunch in the Restaurant Car

When the war came, the meals in English trains realised, as everybody knows, a squalor hitherto unprecedented. The diet rarely varied. There was soup (pea or tomato), fish (cod), cheese (Cheddar) and biscuits, topped off with coffee. All these things tasted exactly alike, that is, they did not taste at all. As the first dreary years of peace succeeded one another, there were from time to time announcements of improvements, improvements intended and improvements achieved. There were new luncheon cars and buffet cars and cars intended to look like old English inns parading shamelessly under such titles as Ye Olde Englishe Rose and Crown. But though waiters might vary their customary uniform with smocks and aprons, though one might sit on stools at buffets, or lounge on bar counters, though one might view the scenery through diamond panes of Tudorfied glass, the food remained incorrigibly the same. There was still tomato soup out of a tin, still cod, still the sausage which tasted of bran served with the Heinz baked beans, still the assorted synthetic cold meats and "meat loaf," still the eternal stewed pears, the everlasting ice, the dry cheese and biscuits. Did I say that the dietary had not varied since the war? I was wrong, shamefully and maliciously wrong, a spiteful detractor of a great British service honestly trying to do its best. The railways now offer richer and more varied fare, fare which improves year by year. For are not the sausages, the Heinz beans, the mixed synthetic cold meats, the pears, and, of course, the sprouts, the cabbages and the potatoes—"Boiled or roast, sir?"—are not these glorious comestibles improvements? Of course they are. How needlessly impertinent of me to forget!

To lunch or dine in a restaurant car still gives people a rather grand feeling. "The journey won't be so bad. You will have lunch in the train", they say to one another hopefully, as they see one another off. And as they leave the carriage for that barbarously early meal—first session 11.30! —I see them look down their pitying noses at me left behind in the compartment. They come back about one, replete with their dabs of fish, gorged with their sausages, puffed up with their little wedges of cheese. Perhaps they have had a "Gin and It" to start off with, perhaps a Bass—or was it a Worthington? All the beers taste alike now—with the meal.

Others in the compartment have brought their lunches with them and are genteely nibbling their sandwiches. This is my moment. Slowly, with a certain ceremony, I proceed to unpack my lunch. If there is room I spread it out on the carriage seat. The sardines, the *pâté*, the slices of veal or pork, the hard boiled egg, the pickled onions, the slices of cold pudding, the cheese. There is the flask of sherry and the half bottle of red wine. Too polite or too awed to comment, they watch me in silence with furtive glances. But I am not to let them off so easily. I want to express myself on the subject of English food, on train lunches and on sandwiches. I desire to make them realise at how small a cost, with how little trouble, they could have eaten how much better a lunch. I tell them of all the things that you have read in this chapter, and to soften the feelings of envious asperity occasioned by this complacent display of gastronomic superiority, I bring out and hand round the thermos containing the hot drink. These are the pleasures of display.

CHAPTER VI

The Pleasures of Hurdles

THERE is a pattern in my life which has recurred so often that I can only conclude that it springs from and reflects some deep-seated element of the self—element or elements, since the pattern is complex, and the threads many. One is a hatred of having things laid on and laid out for me ; another, a spiritual puritanism which makes me incapable of enjoying pleasures that I haven't earned, earned by some preliminary exercise of effort involving some difficulty, some patience of endurance, even a little risk. In short, I am required to surmount the hurdle of ordeal before I am permitted to browse in the pastures of delight. Since this, which I have called the puritanical, is the most continuous and distinctive in this complex pattern, I have entitled this chapter "The Pleasures of Hurdles." An aversion from cars constitutes a second thread. I suspect that there is something pathological here, the implications of which I am not sufficiently expert in empirical self-knowledge to determine. Be that as it may, I propose to regard the car or, more precisely, my feeling of aversion from the car as the accident and the surmounting of the hurdle as the essence of these occasions. But enough of generalities ; let me give some examples.

Arrival for Country Weekend

I am to stay for the weekend at a country house. The hostess sends in advance a time-table and recommends trains. "Come," she says, "by one or other of these and you will be met in the car." And, she may add, "The so-and-so's will be travelling down at the same time, so you will have company." Or, if the house is in the Home Counties, "The so-and-so's will be driving down. I am asking them to ring you up and arrange to pick you up in Town so that you can come down with them."

That is enough for me. The thought of Liverpool Street or Waterloo at one o'clock on a Saturday, the prospect of finding or being found by smartish people on the train, of having to talk to them during the journey, so that I cannot read my book, of being met with them at the local station by the car, met between three and three-thirty in the afternoon when it is just too late to be after lunch and just too early to be before tea, so that there is half an hour or so of polite conversation to be got through before one can go out and *do* something, of arriving, moreover, psychologically unprepared, having had no time to myself to sleep in, to read in or simply to "lurk" in, no time, therefore, to collect myself and enter into possession of myself so that I may be fortified against the impact of the weekend company—not to speak of the other accompaniments and consequences of the officially sponsored journey by train—the prospect of all this is intolerable to me.

Even worse is the thought of the company on the drive down in the car through interminable spreading suburbs of the people I am to meet all through the weekend, and of the being decanted at the end of the drive, jaded and low, to get through the hour till tea arrives as best I can.

So what I do is this. I try to find a station which is situated at a distance of not less than six and not more than ten miles from the house[1] and to arrive there at some time between twelve and two. I eat my lunch on the train or at a pub near the station of arrival. I then walk for some three hours or more, arriving at the weekend house somewhere about five o'clock, in time for a latish tea. I like going across country, over ploughed fields and through meadows, and I particularly like going through woods. As a result I am apt to be rather the worse for wear when I reach the house at which I am to stay.

My approach usually takes place through the back

[1] These figures have been gradually reduced with the passing years.

premises. Hence it is as a disreputable looking person crossing a paddock or making his way through a kitchen garden that I first impinge upon the vision of the domestics of the house of my potential host ; or they become aware of me as a man climbing the fence or breaking through the shrubbery which separates farm from garden ; or I emerge from the depths of a wood to burst suddenly upon the startled gaze of the gardener digging the potato patch.

As at the best of times my clothes are below the average standard of persons of my class and income, and as in the course of my cross country walk I have perspired freely, I have got my boots muddy and my person dishevelled, the gardener accosts me as if I were the intruding tramp for whom he takes me. He wants to know what I think I am doing and where going. When I tell him that I am going to tea in the big house he thinks I am insulting him by pulling his leg and is apt to be very angry with me. I find the whole situation diverting in the extreme as I make my way up through the cabbages and potatoes on to the shaven lawn in front of the house and solemnly ring the front door bell, with the angry gardener still baying at my heels. The meeting, as I disappear within the portals, of two social worlds, the merging of two levels of existence, on both of which I have my being, never fails to give me pleasure apart from the peculiar and private pleasure of baiting authority in the person of the gardener.

My arrival, tired and dirty, is an event of interest to the other guests who, having travelled from London in one another's company, are by now thoroughly bored with one another. Moreover, once she has got used to the idea of arrival on foot, the English hostess tends to treat the walker as an object of interest and even respect. "I expect you will be walking," she writes to you on a later occasion, or "I know you prefer walking." There is something romantic as well as English, she feels, in the appearance of the rucksack on the walker's back. Poets, she knows, do or used to do that sort of thing, and vague memories of the literature of walking tours, of Hazlitt and Stevenson and R. Jefferies

74

flit down the muddled corridors of her brain. She presents you as an object of respectable interest to her guests. "Let me introduce you to Dr. Joad," she says. "He has walked all the way from X—— station. He loves walking." And though she herself hasn't walked more than a mile in years, she shows an interest in mileage, times and routes. These serve as subjects of conversation and so, one way and another, my hostess makes a fuss of me and wants to know whether I will have a bath before tea. For her part, she suggests that I should have a cup of tea first, but leaves it to me. I, who have been bored by no company but my own for four or five hours, am delighted to see people. I am in the best of spirits, attentive, amusing, and prepared to be amused. Also I have a first-rate appetite. After tea, a hot bath and a drink I come down to dinner feeling like a god.

School in the Isle of Man

Again, I am, we will suppose, to speak at a School. (But why should I not particularise ? There is nothing disgraceful about what I am to relate, so let me be precise.) I am going, then, to that admirable King William's School in the Isle of Man, whence proceeds the general knowledge paper that every Christmas bedevils and humiliates the learned readers of *The Times*.

I go by air and am met at the airport by my hostess. To me an aeroplane is at once the most boring and the most terrifying of all the modes of travel which human beings have devised for mailing themselves from one part of the earth to another. I arrive, then, at three o'clock, feeling frightened and sick. I look as yellow as I feel. The school is quite close to the airfield and my hostess invites me to a rest, a hot bath and an early cup of tea. No, I say, I must have a bit of a walk in order to get over the aeroplane. "But the school," she insists, "is only a mile or so away." "I know, but please may I have a walk before going there ? " My hostess is surprised and a little disconcerted, but she is a walker herself and yields. We accordingly get into the car and drive to the nearest hill. I walk up it as quickly as I can, desiring only to be by myself, to lie on my back in the heather, to look at the sea and the sky, to hear the curlew, and to let nature cleanse my spirit of the pollution of the beastly plane. I desire these things above everything in the world, even if I am spared only a few minutes for their enjoyment. But my hostess being, as I have said, a walker, wants to climb the hill with me. This is better than nothing, indeed it is very good, but it isn't quite what I want. And so being by now on easy terms with her I explain my difficulty. "I have been working hard in London, full of committees, beset by people," etc., etc. "I long for a little time by myself and tomorrow I would like to do a long walk by myself." What route, I ask, would she suggest?

Now that I have thrown myself upon her merciful understanding, she consents to let me go alone. For tomorrow she suggests, of course, Snaefell. Have I been up it? She dilates on its wildness and grandeur ; it is, for her, the pride of the Island. But it is a long way from the school. "Is there a 'bus ? " I ask. No, there is no 'bus but she is perfectly willing to take me there. I look pleased but doubtful. "Oh, but you want to be by yourself and you are thinking that if I drive you, you will have me with you. You needn't be afraid. I will drop you and go home. I have plenty to do at home." "But how shall I get back in the afternoon ? " "We'll settle where you are to come down and I will fetch you at any time you care to say." Now that, I suggest, is the cream of hospitality in that it pleases the guest in the way in which he wishes to be pleased and not in the way in which his hostess thinks he ought to be pleased. Moreover, it puts the car to its correct use. It takes you where you want to go, drops you and calls for you again when you want to be collected. The trouble is, of course, that most people are in such bondage to their cars that, once you have let yourself be put into the things, they won't let you get out when you want to ; or they will insist on accompanying you. To take you out, to drop you, go home, come out again, collect you and bring you back, entails a very high degree of thoughtful and unselfish consideration. I bless that woman.

Walking in the Middle West

There is an American version of this pattern. You arrive, or, more precisely, I arrive, at some place in the Middle West, frayed, jaded and yellow after a night in one of those dreadful American sleeping cars, sleeping cars without "jerries," so that whenever you are moved to pass water in the night, you have to walk the whole length of the car and then back again, effectively waking yourself and others up in the process. At the station I am met by an effusive American hostess and immediately the resources of the celebrated American hospitality are brought into play. "We will drive up to the house and have some breakfast and then, Professor Joad, I would be pleased to know what you would like to do. You can play 'squash' with my son and then go and have a swim in the bath. Or my daughter will be pleased to take you round the golf course. Or we can go for a trip in the car. Or maybe you are tired after the train and would just like to go and rest." I thank her profusely, decline politely and say that what I would really like to do is to go for a walk.

I see an expression of disbelief, almost of concern, pass over her face. It is just as if I had said something indecent. Displaying hostess's tact, she puts the suggestion behind her. It is as though I hadn't made it.

After breakfast the question comes up again, and again I say that I would like to go for a walk. Again the slight sense of shock ; again the incredulity. But I stick to my guns, apologising for my lapse of good manners by assuring her that no affront is meant, and appealing to the well-known fact that Britishers are mad anyway.

At last I prevail. The car is brought round, we embark and drive solemnly for twenty minutes or so along a perfectly straight road stretching away over a perfectly flat land to infinity. We disembark, park the car beside the road, walk for two or three miles along the road, sustaining a stream of innumerable automobiles and the gaze of their incredulous occupants, turn round and walk two or three miles back again to the waiting car.

77

Why not across country? It is never done. There are bootleggers, share croppers, bandits, man eating tigers and God knows what in the American country—so, at least, one is given to understand. One might stretch a point for a mad visitor and walk along a road. But leave the road? No, not for anybody. So much for walking in America.

Why do I do it? Why insist? The attempt to answer these questions may help me to discover the common thread that runs through the incidents I have described. Why this enormous distaste for the weekend car? Why insist on leaving the car and climbing the hills? Why make such a "to-do," in order to refuse all the good things that the kind Americans have laid on for me, and go instead for a dreary walk?

There are, I think, broadly three reasons, of which the first two are comparatively straightforward, while the third is complicated, being in fact the theme of this chapter.

1. *Dislike of Cars*. I detest cars. It was, I think, in 1908 that an enterprising science master at Blundell's took me for my first drive in a car. It was an open car in which we drove from Tiverton to Sidmouth and back. I was much excited by the prospect and can still remember the disillusion which attended its realisation. When I got back to Tiverton, I was cold, miserable and low spirited. My wits were dulled, my body chilled and heavy, my whole being devitalised.

I have never seen reason to reverse this judgment on my first car experience. The most magnificent Bentley or Rolls in which I have been subsequently driven has moderated its intensity without altering its fundamental quality.

Of the social effects of the car which has transformed our lives and ruined our countryside, I do not here speak. But I can't forbear to put on record the effects of its impact upon my person, if only for the pleasure of expressing my astonishment that nobody but myself seems to feel them. (*a*) Most car journeys are too long and all are longer than you are led to expect. Car drivers persistently under-estimate times and distances. Hence you are almost always driving in an agitated rush for fear lest you be late.

78

(*b*) It is impossible not to drive fast. You may deplore fast driving yourself and denounce it in others. You may say that "speeding" is bad manners—and so it is. You may say that the car enables you to see the country. But you will be wrong. For the agitation of the spirit seals the senses so that you are blind to whatever natural beauties may survive on the roads for the car driver's indifferent eye to rest upon. You will drive slowly, you say, along the country lanes and presently you will get out and walk. But you don't; you speed along country lanes as if they were main roads, and you don't get out.

(*c*) In a car you can neither read, write nor converse and it is only with great difficulty that you can sleep. Presently you sink into a coma in which, incapable of any rational activity of mind or physical activity of body, incapable, in fact, of anything except of continuing to do what you are already doing, you become a passive sufferer of the experiences that the car inflicts upon you. You are not happy ; on the contrary, you are bored, cold and miserable, but at the same time you are so reduced by the car that you dread the thing stopping, dread the exertion of getting up and getting out. That, no doubt, is why car drivers find it so hard to get out and go for a walk.

(*d*) The after-effects are distressing. You arrive all liver and no legs. The perpetual revolutions and explosions of the internal combustion engine have given you a headache and you have no desire for the company of your fellows. A drink is necessary before you are fit for human intercourse, and even then it is low order intercourse. For my part, until I can have a walk, a sleep and a quiet read, or do a little digging in the garden, I am unfit for human society. These are some of the reasons why I prefer to go by train and walk.

2. *Dislike of Rape.* I dislike staying in a place without first making some preliminary acquaintance, however slight, with the surrounding country. To do so, seems to me both discourteous and unnatural. Hence I dislike arriving in the dark and I always try, if I can, to walk up from the

station. I am profoundly interested in and considerably affected by the different and distinctive "feels" and "flavours" of different parts of the countryside. I like, for example, to think that I can detect the difference between east and west Sussex, no less than the differences between Sussex and Hampshire and between Sussex and Kent, which latter differences are profound.

Travelling to a hitherto unvisited part of the country is still, for me, a considerable experience and the approach should, I think, be carried out in form and with circumspection. To drive straight there in a car or to go by train and drive straight from the station is, for me, an unceremonious method of approach. It is a kind of taking by storm without the careful preliminary inspection of maps and calculation of distances which are indispensable preliminaries to what I have called the approach in form, the approach of ceremony. In short, it is rape, and rape of country is only less distasteful than rape of women. Nor, indeed, can love survive so violent an approach.

Long before I taught myself to reflect upon the meaning of this idiosyncrasy of mine and to rationalise it into a doctrine, I had begun to practise it. I can remember, for example, the first visit that I paid to the Black Mountains that lie on the borders of Herefordshire and Monmouthshire. We were to stay at Llanthony Abbey, which had recently been turned into a hotel, in the middle of the mountains. The country was new to me and I was looking forward with the liveliest interest to seeing it.

We started on a Saturday mid-day after a morning's work in the office—all office workers know about this ; the object is not to waste a day's leave on half a day's work—and arrived at Abergavenny just before six. Here we changed on to a local line for Llanvihangel where a car was waiting. After half a day in the train I was wild with energy and all for walking. I persuaded one man to go with me, and, at about half past six of a summer's evening we set off to walk the seven miles or so to Llanthony, climbing a couple of fourteen to fifteen hundred feet ridges on the way.

The Black Mountains are fine and wild, though I have never felt any very great personal affection for them, and we set off at a spanking pace of nearly four miles an hour. Our route lay across country, and before long we lost our way. Then it grew dark and I was frightened. (The coming of darkness when one is out walking in the country always terrifies me.) Finally we fetched up at a farmhouse where we telephoned for a car in which we finished our journey ignominiously and expensively. But during that long and, at times, intimidating walk over new country I had made my Monmouthshire accommodations. My legs were scratched and torn, my hands had been stung by nettles, my feet were covered in mud, my shirt was wet with sweat, but the country had accepted me and I went to sleep tired and contented.

3. *Hurdles.* I come to my third reason which, as I have said, is complex. It comprises two elements which, though owning a common origin, are at least superficially different. The first, which is the source of what I have called "the pleasures of hurdles," takes its rise from the following idiosyncrasy.

I am unable to enjoy any pleasure or to taste any satisfaction, unless I feel that I have first earned it, earned it by some preliminary labour, ardour, risk or endurance. Thus, I don't like drinking before an ordeal as a stimulus, but after it is over as a reward. Hot baths are for me a form of minor self-indulgence to which the Anglo-Saxon race, especially the female part of it, is immoderately addicted. Screaming, gushing, interminably chattering, leaving a background wireless to play day in and day out, leaving their cars standing with their engines running and throbbing, leaving dogs to bark for hours on chains, making, in fact, and tolerating the most brutal and continuous assaults on the sense of hearing, women nevertheless affect an exaggerated niceness in all matters affecting the sense of smell. Not a weekly, but a daily bath they profess to consider the indispensable condition of a minimum hygiene. And so they are always in and out of their baths—there are women who spend half their lives washing the whole of their bodies— and take it for granted that I share their addiction to the extent of desiring to be woken up—"The bathroom's empty now ! "—half an hour before I had intended to rise, in order to share in these ablutionary rites.

I do, indeed, consider the pleasures of the hot bath to be substantial, but I hold that they are not to be partaken of in cold blood for their own sweet sake or for the sake of cleanliness, but only after some preliminary exercise of sweaty effort—five sets, let us say, on the tennis courts or a walk on the tops of the Lakeland hills or half a day's riding in cold driving rain—has earned them. Alternatively, I would hold a bath to be justified for the removal of accumulated dirt of some weeks' standing.

The second element savours of cussedness. It may best be described as a refusal or an inability to take advantage of what has been specially laid out and laid on for me. Here is a fine summer's morning, here the well-stocked library, here the wide desk, the tested penholder, the favoured nib. The house is quiet and there are three hours to go before luncheon. Can I write my best ? I cannot. The favourable circumstances, the knowledge that everything is laid out and laid on militate against the very thing they favour. The wholly unfavourable circumstances in which I *can* write will be described later.

Here, again, is the meeting point of place, time and opportunity, the quiet hotel or country cottage. It is Friday night and the whole weekend lies before us. Can I make love ? I cannot, or can do so only with difficulty, only, as it were, at the last moment. (The untoward circumstances in which I *can* make love will not be described at all.)

Again and again this pattern has repeated itself in my life. Let me illustrate in more detail these dispositions of mine, the disposition, first, to refrain from taking advantage of what is laid out and laid on for me and the disposition, secondly, to seek a hurdle or, if no hurdle is to be found, to erect a hurdle before I can enjoy myself.

On Not Taking Advantage of What Has Been Laid Out and Laid On.

For some years I was connected with Butlin Camps. These have often been described and I don't propose to add here to the descriptions. I content myself with registering my wholehearted approval. Now Butlin Camps are emphatically places where everything *is* laid on, from tennis courts to golf courses, from horse riding on the sands to car riding round the camp, from billiards to shove-ha'penny, from Viennese cafés to Olde Englyshe Innes, from kindergarten schools to dance halls, from cinemas to theatres, from sermons by Bishops to performances by hypnotists, from silence rooms to community singing, from post offices to shops and private railway stations, not forgetting the all-pervading "golden voice" which, waking you at 7.45 in the morning with the admonition to "Be happy today the Butlin way," contrives to encourage, admonish, direct, exhort and inform you every half hour of the day and finally sends you to bed with a perfect fusillade of hearty, treacly goodnights. There are also laid on cars and swimming pools.

Indeed, the laying on of cars has become at Butlin's as traditional a piece of symbolic ceremonial as was in other ages and places the laying on of hands.

Walking to Butlin's

Some six of us, all connected in one way or another with the organising and entertaining of Butlin campers, left the train at York. The ceremonial car was in attendance at the station waiting to take us to the Filey Camp.

I have already explained my objections to arriving at a place in a car and my preference for walking. Here they operated in full force, so that almost from the first moment of entering the vehicle my mind was occupied with the problem, how to persuade my hostess—one of the famous Butlin redcoats, her blazer covered with medals and ribbons—to let me out of the car in order to do a walk of some seven or eight miles into Filey. The difficulties of the undertaking were (*a*) that I didn't know when we should have reached a point some seven or eight miles distant from Filey ; (*b*) that in the atmosphere of deliberate hilarity which prevailed in the car my request would certainly be greeted with derisive incredulity which, being spiritually low and weak from the train and car journeys, I should find it difficult to stand up to ; (*c*) that it was pouring with rain and that it was imperative for me to change some part of my "townee" clothing before getting out to do the walk.

When I made my outrageous proposal, it did, indeed, provoke a sort of fury of incredulity. That they should have thought me mad was only to be expected, but their derision contained a hint of annoyance. Here was the blessed car so thoughtfully laid on for my special benefit and here was I spurning it. Moreover—it is no use denying it—I was proposing to make myself an awful nuisance, since, as it was raining too hard for me to take off my clothes in the road, I had to change, divesting myself of coat and trousers and donning another pair, in the confined space of the car, upsetting and disturbing everybody in the process. The bodily contortions involved in taking off a pair of town shoes and putting on a pair of heavy hob-nailed boots particularly discommoded them. In the course of these operations I trod heavily on our hostess's elegantly shod foot. I must have made myself a devil of a nuisance.

In the end I got out. I had no mackintosh, so, on the principle that my clothes would in any event be wet through in no time and that the fewer of them there were to get wet the better, I set off on the walk clad only in shirt and trousers. For some reason or other I was without a map, but I knew that all I had to do was to walk southwards along the coast until I came to Filey.

The walk proved unexpectedly formidable. The cliffs were intersected by a number of deep valleys or ravines along the bottoms of which streams ran to the sea, necessitating a series of sharp descents and ascents. Worse were the intermittent outbreaks of sporadic builders' rash. There they were, the little red brick horrors with their staring slate roofs ; there, the pink bungalows, the shacks, the Nissen huts, the caravans, the old 'buses and railway carriages scattered all over the cliffs with as much respect for order and tidiness as if a giant had shaken them out of a pepper-pot. Sticking up all over the skyline they looked like the jagged teeth of a dissipated saw or the sparse hairs on an ill-shaved chin. They were so placed that they could not only see over but be seen from over the greatest possible distances, with the result that in proportion to their numbers they devastated a vast area of cliff. As each had allocated to itself as much of the surrounding land as its predatory owner thought proper to enclose, the edge of the cliff was studded with threatening "Private" notices, warning trespassers of their impending prosecution, while the air was made hideous by the barking of a hundred dogs. After a couple of humiliating en-counters with infuriated cliff-polluters I was driven to make detours inland, and finally arrived late in the evening with only just time for a bath, a drink or two in the Viennese Café or the Continental Lounge or the Olde Englyshe Inne or the American Bar before dinner. Having successfully escaped the car and overcome my hurdle, I ate my meal with a conscience as good as my appetite. I felt that I had earned my food and drink and my mind was at rest. I was suffused with inner happiness, a private happiness, a personal happiness, a happiness of the self.

Horror of the Sea

The hosts and hostesses at Butlin's Camps are in one respect like the Americans, they are very hospitable and, as I have said, everything is laid on and laid out for you. I remember arriving one evening at the Clacton Camp. It had been a very hot day and a great wind was blowing in from the east. We arrived just before tea at which the usual suggestions were made for our entertainment. A game of tennis ? They could fit me out with racquet, shoes and ball. A tour of the camp, a ride on the beach—horses were available—a game of billiards, a bathe in the camp pool or just a rest ? Perhaps just a rest would be best.

I was hot and sticky and wanted above everything to bathe. But I thought of the camp swimming pool, filled with hygienically chlorinated water, its air throbbing with relayed crooning, its margin gay with flowers and flags and set with deck chairs in which old men reclined to watch the bodies of young women flirting their swimming suits in the sun, and my "complex" against the synthetic, the ready-made, the artificial, the so elaborately laid on, rose up on its hind legs and revolted. "Thank you very much," I said, "I should like to bathe in the sea."

The effect of my words was not dissimilar from that produced in America by my proposal that I should go for a walk. Again the slight sense of shock, again the suggestion that I had said something indecent, something that it were better not to have heard. Presently the subject came up again—"What would you like to do?" Again I made my improper suggestion. This time they reacted strongly. If I wanted to bathe, why not use the pool? There it was, not twenty yards away, a pool recommended by a dozen considerations, beautifully appointed, hygienically chlorinated, with the chill guaranteed taken off. The sea was cold, the sea was very rough; in fact, the sea was downright dangerous. I should be dashed to pieces by the waves.

"Don't any of you," I asked, "ever bathe in the sea or want to bathe in the sea?" The idea, it appeared, had never occurred to them. "Then why," I asked, "do you, why does everybody insist on going to the seaside? Why are Butlin Camps always planted by the seaside?"

And this is, indeed, a very odd thing whose significance I can't pretend to fathom. The seaside, as we know, is the desired bourne of all holiday makers. The chief feature of the seaside is the sea. Seaside seekers, one might suppose, would therefore wish to enter the sea. They might even be supposed to have come to the seaside for precisely that purpose. But at a Butlin Camp, apparently, they do no such thing.

Moreover, all along the sea front, often situated at no more than a score of yards from the beach, swimming baths dug and equipped at enormous expense invite people to partake of the joys of bathing without entering the sea. Why? What is the motive behind this substitution of pools for sea? And what is the reason for the obstacles which impede the efforts of the would-be sea bather? Why, for example, do the local authorities of seaside places exact a price for entrance to the sea, forbidding him to undress upon the beach and then making him pay through the nose for the use of a tent or hut and costume?

We are driven, I think, to the conclusion that there exists a real preference for the artificial, the synthetic, the deliberately manufactured and laid on as compared with the natural, the primitive and the given. (Yet even the sea, I suppose, must have been "laid on" by the Creator.)

Not sharing this preference, I insisted, to the scandal of my hosts, on bathing in the sea. Accompanied by a group of officials and watched by a crowd of astonished sightseers I traversed the fifty yards or so separating the Camp boundary from the seashore, and entered the forbidden element. I was dashed about by the waves and enjoyed myself very much, but the chief cause of my enjoyment was the pleasure, the purely private and personal pleasure which I derived from not taking advantage of what had been laid on.

And yet, as I have hinted above, this is far from being a complete account of the complex condition of enjoyment that this experience engendered. For the pleasure of not taking advantage of the "laid on" shades by insensible degrees into the pleasure of overcoming the difficulties of the "not laid on", the pleasure, in short, of doing the difficult thing and so, and only so, of earning the enjoyment which comes when the difficult thing has been accomplished.

On Being Deliberately Late for Trains

I remember a day spent climbing the Brecon Beacons. I was already fattening into late middle age and to drag myself, after a considerable preliminary walk, to the top was about as much as I could manage. We were to take the train back to Brecon from a place called Torpanto and we had time enough for the three or four miles, all of them down hill, to the station. In fact more time than enough, so that it suddenly came to me that the thing was too easy. Seized with an impulse to make it arduous, I suddenly plunged down the mountain side and, ignoring the protests of my companions, younger and physically infinitely more competent than myself, made off as fast as I could in the opposite direction. I climbed another ridge and, running down the hillside, came at the bottom upon a lake, private, I think, but deserted. I threw off my clothes and plunged in.

When I was rejoined by my protestant friends some miles further on, it was obvious that we had only just time to catch the train. In fact, we had to run for it, run for a couple of miles and, as I began to lag, one of us ran on ahead to meet the train as it came into the station and hold it there for the two or three minutes that it took me to come panting up.

Why, I was asked, had I so gratuitously insisted on this unnecessary rush ? Unable at short notice and with no breath to initiate my friends into the mysteries of "hurdle erection", I had no alternative but to leave them under the impression that I was the victim of a tiresome caprice. And perhaps, after all, it is to this and to nothing more that "hurdle erection" amounts.

So, too, when visiting a daughter at Oxford, I have insisted on dragging her out for an all-day walk into the strictly preserved Wytham Woods with hazards of game-keeper and certainty of arriving back late, muddy and exhausted for the Oxford evening engagement, rather than constrain myself to lounging through the day, the all too easy and agreeable Oxford day which offered itself so obviously and alluringly with its drinks, its lunch and its stroll by the river. Somehow, I felt, I must invest my day at Oxford with significance, and lacking any other device submitted my daughter and myself to the rather pointless ardours and endurances of a rushed expedition to Wytham in the rain.

THE PLEASURES OF HURDLES

And here, I see, I am passing by a natural transition from the refusal to take advantage of the thing laid on to the deliberate erection of hurdles to make things difficult, from, in fact, the negative to the positive aspect of what is at bottom the same state of mind, the common source of these allied pleasures. So let me mark the transition by proceeding officially, as it were, to an exposition of the pleasures of hurdles.

The Conditions of Writing

Since writing is among my professions, I will begin by instancing the application of the principle of hurdles to writing. At home, as I have said, everything is laid on for writing. My library is filled with books—four thousand of them. Here are not only all the books I could ever want to read, but all the books I could have need to refer to ; the *Authors' and Printers' Dictionary*, so useful—it tells you just what you want to know and no more—the *Who's Who*, the *Dictionary of Quotations*, the *Collection of Aphorisms*, the *A.B.C.* . . . Here is my desk just the right height, just the right size, its drawers containing just that collection of objects of stationery—the bulging penholder, the relief nibs, the Koh-i-Noor pencils, the green blotting paper, the pins (not paper clips) for attaching papers, the envelopes large and small (with a special drawer for used envelopes—one of my old-man economies—of every shape and size with the gum still adhering and a bottle of paste on the shelf to supply its place if it has worn away), the various sizes of notepaper, the drawer full of scrap paper. Here is my revolving chair to be screwed to the exact height that I require. (I am fussy about this. Most chairs and tables are unsuited to the writer, the chair being too high, the table too low, so that he must bend over and bend down when he writes, subjecting himself to strain and causing the blood to run into his eyes. This is true of almost all dining room tables, since for eating you require a lower level than is suitable for writing. Almost all tables other than dining tables are spindly and shaky. So are most so-called writing desks which, moreover, lack any central aperture into which to stow the legs. The tools which the writer needs to ply his trade are very few, a solid table or stable desk with plenty of arm-space and a chair of suitable height. It is surprising how rarely they are forthcoming.) To my left is the window so that the light falls over my left shoulder. (If the window is in front of you, the light dazzles the eye and dazes the brain ; if to the right, the writing hand comes between the page and the light and casts its shadow on the page.) The window looks out on to a garden sufficiently large to guarantee a reasonable degree of quiet by interposing a substantial distance between my desk and children, barking dogs, neighbours' gramophones and wirelesses, and the knocking and hammering of building or repairing workmen.

On the whole I have been lucky at Hampstead in respect of this prime necessity of silence. Everything here is laid on for writing, everything is "just so", and, being "just so", it ensures at least a reasonable flow of words.

Subject the body of the writer to the same physical conditions day after day and the mind will become conditioned to function in the way which the conditions suggest, that is, in the present instance to expressing its ideas on paper. Hence I endeavour to sit down to the same desk in the same chair at the same hour every morning, having risen, drunk my cup of tea, opened the letters, read the paper, played the pianola for half an hour and been to the lavatory. Regularity in these matters is commended by all who study the welfare of their bodies and desire the free working of their bowels. It seems reasonable, in the circumstances, to expect the mind to shed its surplus products on the desk as the body has just shed *its* in the lavatory. And so on the whole it does ; so, indeed, it should. If at my time of life I hadn't discovered what suits me, I should be a fool indeed, and for ordinary workaday purposes these conditions I have so carefully laid on serve well enough.

But for writing abundantly, writing with ease and inspiration, writing as a pleasure and not as a duty, I demand something more.

Pleasure of the Stolen Minutes

I have been travelling this morning from Ipswich to London. The train is on time and there is half an hour to wait before my London appointment. No time to go home ; no time to go anywhere else. I go, then, straight to the waiting room of Liverpool Street Station. Hideously ugly, utterly bleak, it conforms admirably to type. The walls are painted green and brown. Upon them hang coloured prints of places served by the old G.E.R. Round them run horsehair seated benches. In the centre is a solid, deal table. There are a timetable of suburban and a timetable of main line departures. Sometimes there is a gas fire. And that is all—literally all—except, of course, for the people who continually come and go, imposing themselves upon the attention with clattering footsteps, swinging doors and conversations incidental to arrivals and departures, any one of which would in other circumstances send me demented. Babies cry and squall ; children play ; an old man near me belches meditatively ; a mother sitting at the central table is noisily administering food to her child ; outside one window engines come and go and whistle and shriek ; outside the other taxis draw up. Nothing, in fact, is laid on, everything militates against the concentration and expression of thought.

Yet these so untoward circumstances suit me exactly. They constitute a hurdle, not a hurdle self-erected but a hurdle self-sought. I know in advance that I shall be able to write in the waiting room precisely because the circumstances *are* difficult and unfavourable and also because I have only half an hour to write in. If I had a great space and a vacant time, if, in fact, I had the whole morning at my disposal, I should moon and doodle on the page and probably write less than in the stolen half hour. But then I couldn't tolerate a whole morning in the Liverpool Street waiting room.

Here, then, are three pleasures of the self, the pleasure of the hurdle, the pleasure of the stolen minutes, and the pleasure of complacency. Other people, I say to myself, would have been put off by these circumstances ; but not I.

Other people would have wasted that half hour ; but not I. I am pleased and proud of myself on both counts.

In pursuit of these pleasures I have come to know with some intimacy the waiting rooms of most of the Southern London termini. All are equally stimulating in respect of their discomfort, but that at Charing Cross, abutting as it does on the pavement where porters whistle and people clamour for taxis is the most highly prized, precisely because it is the noisiest and most uncomfortable. (That at Victoria is the quietest.)

I have added to the pleasure of the stolen minutes by eating meals in these places, thus obviating both the restaurant car on the train and the restaurant in the station. In a restaurant you can never write while you eat, and it is but rarely that you can read. Eating my lunch in the waiting room or on the platform seat—Waterloo is a station very well provided in the matter of platform seats—I can do both. Besides, I get a better lunch.[1]

Timetable of Visit to Kingswood

For many years I observed a regular "hurdle" routine which began in the waiting room at Charing Cross Station. As it illustrates both the pleasures of hurdles, in point of fact of two of them, and the pleasure of the stolen minutes, I venture to describe it in some little detail. I was, then, for a number of years in the habit of visiting a friend who lived at Kingswood in Surrey. I would do a morning's writing at Hampstead and arrive about 1.30 at Charing Cross whence, during the middle of the day, though not in the mornings and evenings, Kingswood is approached.

I would buy fruit at the shop outside the station, go to the waiting room, eat my lunch, eked out with a flask of wine and the newly bought fruit and start to read a book. Because I am enough of a time-miser to want to make the most of my minutes, and enough of a Puritan to think that the pleasures of the afternoon off should not be completely pleasant or, rather, that their pleasantness should be paid

---

1. See Chapter v., pages 67-69 for The Pleasures of Outdoor Food.

for by the expenditure of a certain amount of effort and
endeavour, the book is, if I can so contrive it, a book for
review. I would catch the 2.4 train, finish my lunch in the
train and begin to make notes on the blank pages so thoughtfully inserted by publishers at the end of review books—I
suppose they hope that all books will be review books—so
that I shall be able to write at least *something* about it directly
the train stops. (I can't, unfortunately, write when the train
is going. I have tried hard to teach myself this enviable
accomplishment, but my handwriting, at all times unreadable save by myself, becomes, if I write in moving trains,
unreadable even by me.)

The Wood

At 2.46 I would get out at Chipstead, ascend the down
which lies west and a little south of the station and prepare
to surmount my two hurdles. The first hurdle was the entry
into Banstead Wood. This is, or was, a first class wood.
Its trees are varied ; it blazes with flowers, the bluebells
in spring being particularly notable, and it is full of birds.
During most of the period of my acquaintance with it,
extending for about twenty years, it had been preserved for
pheasants. Recently it has become part of the Green Belt
and now, I believe, belongs to the L.C.C. who have turned
the big house at the far side of the wood into some kind of
institution. A public footpath runs along the outside of the
wood over the down to Kingswood. But this was too
frequented for my purposes ; moreover, to have walked
peaceably along it would have deprived me of my first
hurdle. Besides, I loved actually being in the wood. Being
in the wood meant climbing the fence that ran round it and
this climbing was, in fact, my first hurdle. It doesn't,
I know, sound formidable but in point of fact it was something of an undertaking, since each successive owner of the
property tended to strengthen the fence anew. For the most
part it consisted of high chestnut palings linked with wire at
the top. At one point, however, there was a locked gate
which for years served as my point of ingress, since I could

just hoist myself up by means of a bar which ran laterally along the top of the gate. A drawback to this method was that the gate was insecure on its hinges and swayed abominably under my weight.

As the years passed, I grew fat and heavy and it was only with the greatest difficulty that my increasingly unwieldy body heaved itself over the top. The barbed wire which ran along the top was apt to tear my hands and once badly ripped my trousers.

Once in the wood, I made for the scene of my second hurdle, a particular seat in a particular ride under a particular tree where I would sit down to write for not less than half and not more than three-quarters of an hour. My writing usually took the form of reviewing the book that I had read in the waiting room and in the train. The hurdle principle involved the production of a certain number of words—in point of fact, six hundred and twenty covering two sheets of my note-book—before I allowed myself to stop, and I would aim at writing a substantial part of the review, even if I didn't finish it.

I possess the enviable faculty of being able to fall in a couple of minutes into a fairly profound sleep immediately after lunch whenever I want to do so, and if it was a hot day, I would usually permit myself a quarter of an hour's sleep before beginning. All round me the ground was covered with bluebells, above my head were the spreading branches of an ash, opposite was an oak out of one of the branches of which somebody had carved a lifelike representation of a pheasant. Having slept and written my allotted quota of words, I enjoyed for a moment an almost complete contentment. For most of the obstacles which normally disturb it were absent. For the moment my restless ambition was stilled. Here in the wood I could further none of my projects. I could promote no increase of power or wealth or fame, and for the remainder of the afternoon I contrived to put all three out of my mind. Above all, I had done my allotted piece of work, reviewed my book, surmounted my hurdles and earned my pleasure.

Meanwhile the influences of the peaceful, quiet place had their effect. Some emanation had seeped into me from my environment bringing rest to my unquiet spirit. The fact that the place was known and familiar played no small part in my mood. I felt utterly at home here, expected, welcomed and, because expected and welcomed, calmed and rested.

The Awareness of the Self

And just because desire and ambition *were* stilled, I became aware on these occasions, intensely aware of my own personality; I entered into myself and possessed it. Most of the writings that I have read on meditation and contemplation suggest that individuality is derivative and impermanent. It is, they imply, an incidental though necessary accompaniment of the habitation of the soul in a body ; or it is an attribute of our fallen state ; or it is built up of a congeries of psychological compounds. And, because it *is* derivative and impermanent, when the conditions which normally call it into existence and emphasise its being are absent or in abeyance, it ceases to intrude itself. It is the spirit that now comes to the fore, and unlike the body or the mind, the spirit is in some sense continuous with something greater than itself, the universal spirit or the collective unconscious or the life force or God—at any rate it is continuous with something that is not ourselves, of which our individualities are only incidental expressions. Such is the general tenor of the mystical writings I have read. Such the teaching of Aldous Huxley whom I regard in these matters with respect bordering on reverence.

I can only say that I have not found it so. For me this moment of serenity and absorbed contentment is a moment of intense self awareness. It is my own familiar and wholly undesirable personality that occupies my consciousness, but my personality purged for the moment of its undesirability. These moments bring with them a double conviction ; a conviction first of the permanence, indeed, of the eternity, of the self and, secondly, of what might be called the inner

truth of the experience that so represents it. I am convinced
—with a conviction in which the intellect plays little part—
that here, for once, I am seeing or rather, feeling things as
they are. But I wander from hurdles.

There is one more before I leave the wood, but as it is
potential rather than actual I haven't included it in my list.
It is the hurdle of the keepers. During some part of its
career or, rather, of my career in it, the wood, as I have
already remarked, has been strictly preserved for pheasants.
The inevitable accompaniments of pheasant preserving, the
coops, the scatterings of buckwheat, the melancholy rows
of corpses of birds and little animals—stoats and weasels
and magpies and jays, strung along lines stretched between
the trees—tauten the mind to the constant expectation of
meeting a keeper.

I have several methods of dealing with keepers which I
have set out in detail in another place.[1] They include
running away, bluffing, assuming the personality of a puta-
tive owner or wood inspector, bribing and browbeating,
which last entails taking the initiative and attacking before
being attacked. There is also the appeal to understanding—
pity. This last, I find, can be most effectively made in
one's *rôle* of a writer. "I have something rather difficult,"
I tell him, "to write"—I have even on occasion talked the
keeper and myself into my being a poet—"and I want quiet
and the assurance of not being disturbed. I knew," I tell
him, "that I should enjoy these in the wood, so I came here
to write and the place has, indeed, given me just what I
wanted of it. Look," I would say, holding up the page,
"Look what a lot I have written."

With many keepers this works well enough. They may
even feel a little flattered at the thought of housing a writer
in their wood and being complimented on having kept it
quiet for him, and they let you stay or, even if they move
you on, walk and chat with you until you are out of the
wood. I have employed this method on several occasions
in Banstead Wood.

1. See *The Book of Joad*, Ch. viii.

But here I have also availed myself of an additional method suggested by the circumstances and appropriate only to them. Knowing that the wood was changing, or was about to change hands, I have given myself out to be a representative of the new, the forthcoming, owner. As on the last occasion the place was taken over by the L.C.C., I have been a Forestry Officer of the L.C.C. I know just enough about trees and birds and country matters generally to be able to carry this off, and have had prolonged and elaborate conversations with the keeper on methods of preserving trees, of protecting bark against rabbits, of treating young conifers and even, God help me, on how these horrible trees can be most effectively planted with a view to rapid growth. We have discussed what kinds of fencing will give the best results for the least money and have decided—again, God help me—that those dreadful concrete posts joined with diamond mesh wire netting constitute the best protection against trespassers.

In extenuation I can only plead that pheasant preserving is an abomination, that keepers are the natural enemies of all good men, that I did the keeper no harm and that I derived an intense secret pleasure from these schoolboy escapades, a pleasure private and personal, a pleasure of the self.

Here, then, were two pleasures of the afternoon, the first the pleasure of hurdles—certain, for I don't remember an occasion when I failed to surmount them ; the loss of morale involved by such failure would have been greater than I had the courage to face—the second, the pleasure of keeper-baiting, although this was potential only. It might happen or it might not. On the whole I hoped and, as I grew older, prayed that it might not happen. The two hurdles were quite enough for an afternoon.

CHAPTER VII

The Pleasures of Escape and of the Hobby Horse

THE south-east corner of England—more particularly of Kent and of Sussex running west to Winchelsea—has a character of its own. It is, for example, drier and the air is more exhilarating than anywhere else in the South. You wake up in the morning feeling like ten men or, alternatively, like a king among men, according to whether you are accustomed to reckon in terms of quantity or quality. Everything seems possible, everything seems worth attempting. What is more, you are convinced that, if you attempt it, you will almost certainly bring it off and that if you don't it doesn't much matter. You look out of the window and you find even the sea, even that dull grey expanse of choppy, meaningless water exhilarating. As you dress, you find that you are whistling ; in your bath, if you have one, you sing ; and if anybody were to ask you why you do these things, you couldn't tell him. For they serve no end external to themselves. They are expressions of pure, motiveless impulse.

Like, I suppose, most other people—but the supposition *ex hypothesi* can never be verified—I have my own private forms of impulse-expression, chief among them being hugging myself, jumping up and down, squeaking with pleasure and addressing myself. What do I say ? That, I think, is a question which even in a book devoted to the pleasures of the self must remain unanswered.

The simplest activities, going out to fetch the paper, reading it on the lawn, throwing sticks for the dog to fetch, throwing stones at bottles set on groins, are sources of profound pleasure. You enjoy passing the time of day ; you revel in the most commonplace observations ; you welcome with affection persons to whom you are totally indifferent. By the afternoon the mood has faded, and at ten you are dog tired, yawn over your book and go early to bed. For the rest, your skin is dry, your sexual temperature low ; you have a vast appetite and a tendency to constipation. The activity of your body is matched by that of your mind, but the mind's activity is on a practical, everyday sort of level. You can do cross-words, get your accounts right, set your affairs in order and play a good game of chess. But the deeper levels are inaccessible ; your mind neither wanders nor day-dreams ; but equally it is without inspiration, nor is it touched by any grace of beauty or insight. Nothing untoward or surprising ever seems to outcrop into your clearly defined consciousness. The unconscious, in fact, might not exist and I should imagine that psycho-analysts who, as I suppose, do very well for themselves in the danker, lusher counties, in the Thames valley for example, or the New Forest, here have difficulty in making a living.

Once the coast has been left behind, this part of England seems to me unattractive. It tends to be flat and, though there are wild, open spaces running on to Dungeness and on Romney Marsh, marshland has little attraction for the visitor. You must *live* in the marsh to feel its hold. . . . The marsh, too, is fringed with the usual scurf of angry, little, red houses.

Sea Front at Hythe

So are the sea fronts. Take Hythe, for example. It exhibits in a peculiar degree all those characteristics which have made the English seaside place at once the wonder and the horror of the world. A long row of buildings consisting almost entirely of hotels and boarding houses lines the front. Unplanned, they are of all sizes, shapes and colours, but most of them have been deliberately encrusted with ornaments, so that balls and knobs and spikes and turrets and gables bunch and cluster and project in every direction like excrescences on the reddened face of the drunkard. The houses stare across the promenade at the sea. The promenade, a long paved walk, runs between the road, along which the motors hurl themselves, and the beach.

There is nothing on the promenade but seats, and nothing on the beach but pebbles. The beach, in fact, is about as unaccommodating to the would-be sitter as could well be imagined. There is no sand for children to dig in or to run on or play cricket and hockey on. There are no rocks to clamber over and no pools left by the receding tide to poke about in. There are no cliffs where the old can sit and enjoy the view. In fact, there is nothing at all but a shelving bank of pebbles intersected by an occasional groin. There is neither shelter from the wind, nor shelter from the sun and the pebbles are the devil to sit on. In fact, a drearier and more unaccommodating stretch of beach it would be difficult to imagine. What, I wondered for the hundredth time as I dragged myself painfully along the hard promenade, do people do in these places ?

Thrombosis

What was I doing ? I was learning to walk. I had been suffering from thrombosis—shall I, I sometimes wonder, ever cease to suffer from it ?—and having lain supine for some weeks I had come to Hythe with my stiff leg to be "pepped up" into health again. I could not have chosen a worse place. The tonic air did in fact "pep" me "up" until I could scarcely contain the energy with which I was bursting, all my usual occupations, riding, tennis, above all walking, being put out of court by my inoperative leg. Let me but walk a hundred yards and it swelled to the size of a bloated, sausage balloon and throbbed like a petrol engine. I simply had to sit down ; so I descended to the beach and, placing myself on the unaccommodating pebbles, stared miserably at the heaving sea, wondering, as I looked at it, why God had made so much of it. The sea is all very well in reasonable quantities, but having shown that He could do the thing, you wouldn't have thought that He would have been so proud of it that He would want to go on repeating the trick for over two-thirds—or is it three-quarters ?—of the earth's surface. For one bit of sea is so very like another bit. Why then, one wonders, so much of it ? I often have the same thought in regard to Americans. Why did God make so many ?

My only form of physical exercise was eating, but even this had its drawbacks. I am one of those who take a long time over my meals and eat very fast and my appetite, at all times large, was sharpened by the tonic air into making upon the available food supply demands which no English hotel, with its carefully calculated bits of bacon, saucers of sugar, dabs of butter and fragments of meat, could possibly implement. I thought continually of food, pondering long and gloomily on prisons, hospitals, concentration camps and other places where people don't get enough to eat. I can only assimilate the amount of food which I consume without turning it into fat by taking prodigious quantities of exercise. Now I was no more able to work off my food than my energy and waxed grossly.

The Seaside

Having been brought up in seaside resorts, I have avoided them ever since my childhood. Viewing one of them now at leisure with an adult and dispassionate eye, I was at a loss to understand what English people can see in them. If they are hearty and vulgar, why do they not go to Hampstead Heath, which is both nearer and cheaper ? If they desire company and amusement at a slightly higher level, why not a Butlin Camp ? If they want games, why not go to the golf course, the tennis court and the bowling green ? If they wish to walk, why not to mountains and moorlands ? Why go to a place where there is nowhere to walk except upon pebbles and the promenade ? If they have any pretensions to taste, why choose these cultural deserts with nothing but the cinema or the concert party on the pier to amuse them in the evening ? Are there no cinemas in London ?

Some attraction for invalids might perhaps be found in the boredom of these places, for boredom, I am led to believe, is an ingredient in health, and seaside resorts with their total lack of reasonable occupation are above all things boring. Bored on the promenade, bored on the pier, bored at the cinema, bored talking genteelly over cups of coffee in the hotel lounge, driven almost melancholy mad for want of somebody to argue with, some hard and unremitting labour to perform—oh, for a good game of chess or bridge, for an article to write, or lecture to give or attend, a book on philosophy to read, oh, for anything rather than the hard pebbles and the soft conversation—I grew very healthy indeed, but health, I thought, was not enough. I wanted something to be healthy *for*. Was I, I asked myself, sent into the world merely to perform the mechanical operations involved in turning good, healthy nourishment into rather inefficient manure, to be, in fact, a low grade fertiliser ? But granted that boredom is good for the body which thrives on the mind's vacuity, granted that boredom has something to do with the alleged health-giving properties of seaside places, I doubt, even so, if that is why people go to them. I have yet to see a "Come to Broadstairs. It is so boring" advertisement.

Probably, I concluded, there is no reason why people go to these places except that everybody else goes there and that they always have gone there. People are, in fact, so little adept at the art of living, they know so little what they need from life, or of the possibilities that life holds in store that they are prepared to accept as pleasures whatever custom prescribes for them and persuade themselves that they enjoy their fortnight at the seaside for no other reason than that they have been hypnotised into believing that they ought to enjoy it.

It was not always so. The seaside myth is, indeed, of comparatively recent origin. Listen, for example, to Mr. Woodhouse in *Emma* commending Cromer in preference to Southend : "And by what I understand, you might have had lodgings there quite away from the sea—a quarter of a mile off, very comfortable."

The seaside. Oh, the dreariness of those soul-depressing words ! For my part, barring extreme cases like the Sahara Desert and the ice floes that surround the North Pole, I consider that there is more to be seen, more to catch the eye, to titilate the nose, intrigue the ear and stimulate the mind in a hundred square feet of earth than a hundred square miles of sea, and I would willingly turn my back on all the watery wastes on the one side of me and all the terra cotta lodging houses on the other in order to look at a cabbage patch.

The Escape—Southsea and Teignmouth

And that precisely is what I did. Whenever previously I had found myself by some mischance in a seaside place, I had straightway set myself to discover means of escape. One of my children was brought up by her grandparents in a hotel at Southsea, and occasionally at weekends I would go down to see her. I would take a train to Sussex early on Saturday morning or late on Friday night, walk for the best part of Saturday in that noble and at that time unknown country—unknown, that is to say, to Londoners—behind Chichester, Bow Hill, Kingley Vale with its yews, Chilgrove, and the little pub at Hook's Way where nobody goes (or went), arrive about seven o'clock still glorying in Sussex and hating Southsea, creep guiltily to my bedroom for fear my mother should catch me and make her usual fuss over my scallywag clothes and muddy boots, and turn up in evening dress just in time for a drink before dinner.

The following morning I would have an early breakfast, collect the daughter and take a Southdown 'bus along that long, dreary road that leads out through Fratton and Cosham and over Portsdown Hill and so through Waterlooville and I know not what other horrors, until at last it reaches the country somewhere near Horndean. We would go for a walk, returning about 1.15, late for Sunday dinner—the highlight, this, of the hotel week—with muddy boots and clothing stained or torn. My unfortunate daughter, who could certainly not be blamed for my vagaries, was violently rated and I received black looks. Why, I was asked, did I have to rush away like that. Couldn't I be content in Southsea even for a morning? My people liked it, other people liked it and thought it very fine. "Look", I was bidden, "at the numbers living in this very hotel. Look at the lovely open common, the dry promenade, the shelters from the wind, the good 'bus services, the numerous cafés for 'elevenses'. What more could anybody want?" But I couldn't explain.

When I was already ageing, fattening and past much walking, I spent a couple of weeks in midwinter at Teignmouth. I reasoned as follows : the places to which I normally went for holidays were wild. They were mountains and moorlands, wide and open, stimulating to the mind and exhilarating to the spirit, provided always that you could walk in them or climb in them or ride in them. But I was getting past these things. I could still walk and ride ; I could still "go up" a mild mountain, but I wanted to be able to choose my time, place and weather. I had recently had a miserable time in the Highlands ; the rain, cloud and fog were continuous and I was mewed up in a wretched, little hotel whose total lack of comfort reminded me that I was getting old. The time, then, had come when, I felt, I didn't want to exert myself simply because there was no alternative to exercise. I wanted a place comfortable, roomy and warm where I could read and write undisturbed and walk only when I wanted to walk. About this time I read an essay by, I think, Max on the pleasures of English seaside places in the depths of winter. He dilated on the sense of space and emptiness, the suggestion of melancholy and the feeling of distinction conferred by the pleased hotel proprietor and the deferential waiters. He praised the solitude.

Accordingly, I chose Teignmouth. I suppose that as a seaside place Teignmouth was well enough. Certainly it contained many pleasant people who asked me out and made much of me. But, alas, the usual thing happened. I could not content myself by the sea and directly the morning's writing was done, I would go to the 'bus centre, take almost the first 'bus that offered and get away—it scarcely seemed to matter where—so long as it was away from the beach, away from the promenade, away from the hotels and away from the sea. For the sea should not, I think, be looked at full face—it out-faces and out-stares you if you stare at it—but should burst upon the view as you top a rise of the Downs or be caught in a glimpse at the end of a valley running between two hills. I would wander all the afternoon over the hills at the back of Teignmouth, walking across ploughed fields, along neglected tracks running between high hedges or through copses ; or I would lie on the grass reading.

Joy at the Back of Hythe

And now, disabled as I was, I was doing the same thing at Hythe. I couldn't walk more than a couple of hundred yards at most, but that was enough for my purpose which was, once more, to get away from the people and the cafés and the ice-cream sellers and the roller-skating rink and the fun palace and the concert parties, away from the front, away from the sea. The 'bus put me off on the top of a ridge whence one could walk at once on to a stretch of downland—it had, in fact, been used as a golf course before the war—intersected by little valleys and indented with cup-like depressions. The time was April and these were carpeted with anemones, primroses and violets. The cowslips were just beginning. I lay on the grass and positively rolled in it ; I lay on my back and watched a lark ascending step by step the ladder of the sky ; I put my hands into a molehill and scooped up a handful of chalky soil. The damp smell of the freshly turned earth assailed my nostrils. I picked daisies and chewed their stalks. I put blades of grass between my thumbs and blew on them. Presently I prowled about and found a linnet's nest in a gorse bush ; it had three eggs. I looked at the sea some three miles away glistening blue in the sun, and rejoiced in the view. This was the right distance for the sea.

As I did these things, I was filled with an intense satisfaction. I cannot put into words what it is that I felt because the feeling was personal and particular, stretching back, I doubt not, into the roots of my ancestral past. It was the feeling of home-coming of some small creature which, born and nurtured in a land of broken hills and valleys scattered with boulders, set with thorn trees and bracken and watered by small streams, is filled with joy as he returns from an alien environment to the sights and sounds and scents of the place that he knows. Perhaps I had lived in some such place as a peasant or walked here as a shepherd boy tending his flock or even—stretching back further—as a faun who had bathed in the streams, hidden in the bracken and pursued the nymphs. But these are the merest rationalisations of a feeling which slips between the meshes of the net in which I am trying to catch it, for our resources of description are too crude for the trapping of feelings so elusive.

I have met no other man who has experienced quite the same pleasure in escape from the seaside as I have done. There are, of course, many who hate its vulgarities, many who share my conviction of its infinite tedium and there are always those who don't like the sea. But nobody, so far as I have been able to discover, is subject to quite the same combination of influences, some rational and describable, some primitive and indescribable, which in my own case are responsible for the pleasure, at once personal and peculiar, which I regularly experience on escaping from a seaside place to the country behind.

Rye Beautiful and Rye Ugly

After a few days at Hythe my desire for escape grew too great to be borne and I went to Rye. Compared with almost any other place in that part of England, Rye is beautiful. It is old and quiet ; the streets are narrow and cobbled ; there are alleys running between the houses where the cars cannot pass, squares and closes set round gardens filled with flowers and flowering shrubs, and close shaved lawns ; there is also a magnificent church. Part of Rye is still girt by a rampart from which there is a wide view over the far-spreading marsh. But Rye is, alas, surrounded by the usual concentric rings of squalor with which successive generations of moderns have seen fit to obscure it, so that the little core of ancient beauty in the middle is like a small and diminishing nut encased in a coarse and ever-thickening husk. In the foreground are the deposits of the nineteenth century, coal-wharves, railway sidings, gas works, yellow warehouses and little, slummy cottages. Outside them are the peculiar emanations of the twentieth century, garages and generating stations and petrol pumps and a wilderness of pylons, poles and wires, in fact all of the *débris* of the electricity and motor age, set amid rows of staring, little red brick boxes that straggle along the road to Winchelsea.

Perhaps it is the knowledge that it is an anachronism, putting up a losing battle against the influences that would destroy it that makes Rye so conscious of itself. On me it produced an effect of deliberate "archaising", as though it were trying, with its picture postcards, its innumerable guest houses and tea rooms, its genteelly up-stage hotels and its air of shabby yet defiant gentility, to bottle and preserve the rapidly fading aroma of its past.

W—and its Trees

So to W—, which so far has almost wholly escaped progress's withering touch. So far but, I gather, no longer. To the west of the great church is a park in the midst of which stands a fine old house. The park is fringed with great trees, sheep browse its acres, and since it crowns a small hill, it holds a magnificent view over the marsh to the sea. This park, I was told, had recently been bought by "the authorities" who proposed to cut the trees down and to put Council houses in their stead. "Is there, then," I asked, "a great demand for houses in W—? " No, there was not, but in Hastings and elsewhere there was such a demand. It had accordingly been decided to accommodate the overflowing populations of these places in the surrounding neighbourhood and W— must take its share of the overflow. Even W—, it was intimated, "must march with the times." Besides there was this magnificent view over the marsh and why should it be enjoyed by the few people, mostly old ladies, who had hitherto lived there ? Why should not the workers who would dwell in the Council cottages be made free of this wealth of natural beauty ? Enough of privilege !

Also (unspoken) the Council houses would spoil the view of the old ladies, let down the general status of the neighbourhood, humble the haughty, dissipate the class atmosphere which still lurked in these semi-feudal old places and so constitute a further instalment of the advance to that blessed condition of equality when the valleys shall be raised up and the mountains brought low and the benefits and beauties of the Welfare State will be enjoyed alike by all. And if the beauty, the charm, the precious distillation of centuries which is the atmosphere of W— were destroyed in the process—well, just look at this beautiful new motor road, with its frequent 'buses affording unlimited and un-precedented possibilities for getting rapidly away from W—.

On these contentions I have several comments and since their subject, the desecration of natural beauty, forms one of the continuing themes of my discourse, a theme upon which, as I grow older, I dilate with ever increasing queru-lousness and at ever greater length, I may justly relate what I am about to say to the general theme of this book by entitling this section the "Pleasures of the Hobby Horse."

PLEASURES OF THE *HOBBY HORSE*

1. *Old Ladies, Old Towns and Views*. It gives me pleasure, then, to point out in the first place that the discomfiture of the old ladies proceeds from nothing better than spite and the desire for revenge. There are the old ladies living in retirement at W—, and there they have been these thirty or forty years past doing, so far as I can see, no harm to anybody even if they don't do any good. Admittedly they are among the representatives of a dying class, but they might, I should have thought, have been allowed to die in peace. The construction of rows of Council houses will destroy their pleasure in W— just as it will destroy my

pleasure in W—. It will destroy theirs, because they will feel that the social tone of the place has been lowered ; it will destroy mine, because it is beauty, sheer, useless, indefensible beauty that will be wantonly sacrificed to class spite.

The argument that W— should take its share of the overflowing population of Hastings, or wherever it may be, is nonsense. Few, if any, of the people who are brought to live here will work here. They will travel some seven or eight miles to their work on motor 'bus or bike, aggravating the transport problem and spending the best part of two hours out of every twenty-four being mailed about over the surface of the earth for all the world as if they were parcels. They will be victims of that unique modern heresy, the heresy, namely, that the mere alteration of the position of the body in space is a good in itself.

Meanwhile, most of what makes W— distinctive will be diminished or abolished in the interests of the creed that whatever of the old and, therefore, the distinctive survives, should be flattened out in order that everything everywhere should be caused to look as alike as possible, the same tarmac roads, the same pink slate-roofed houses, the same bunches of poles joined together by the same wires, the same telephone booths, the same garages, the same canned music, the same wireless, the same dresses and the same girls.

It is hard enough in any event in these days of universal levelling, for places that have come down to us from a more gracious past to maintain the characteristics in which their distinctiveness resides. Circumstance, as usual on the side of the big battalions, has done what it can to assist the process of ironing out. The Temple was distinctive, so it was selected for Hitler's bombs. Oxford was distinctive, so it was selected for the birthplace of Morris, who has turned it into the Latin Quarter of Cowley. Bath is distinctive, and circumstance has decreed that uranium should be discovered under its earth, so that I make no doubt that in fifty years much of Bath will have been undermined from below—if it has not been destroyed from above—to get at the uranium.

I say "circumstance", but I am afraid that what I mean is Providence. It was Providence that let the bombs fall upon the Temple as if there were no Peckham or Harlesden to receive them, Providence that sent Morris into the world at Oxford, as if there were no Coventry or Corby to provide him with a fitting birthplace ; it is Providence that permits the uranium to be discovered under Bath, as if there were no Middlesbrough to be dug up. When it is remembered that what makes these places distinctive is also what makes them beautiful, and that if anywhere in a city there is something different or rare or beautiful, a crescent or a square of houses, a public building, a cobbled street, a church, an old wall, something in which the townsfolk take a pride so that they mention it in their guide-books, speak of it to their visitors and take them to see it, then you may bet your boots that it will be not less than two hundred years old— when, I say, it is remembered how beauty in our age is destroyed and betrayed by man—one might have expected a little favoured treatment from Providence. Providence, one feels, might have done better than to follow so submissively in twentieth-century man's footsteps.

As to the argument that since a view is good all should enjoy it, it proceeds from one of the major heresies of our time, namely, that all goods are quantitative ; therefore, the more of them or, more precisely, the more people who enjoy them, the better. Since to dwell as a member of a family in one room and to have an empty stomach are "bad" and since to multiply houses and food is, therefore, "good", and since we live in an age which interprets "good" in terms of the needs of the common man, that is to say, in terms of houses and food and pools and employment, and since houses, food, pools and employment are all capable of quantitative multiplication, it comes to be believed that *all* goods are capable of quantitative multiplication from which it is concluded that the more people who enjoy them, the better. But this conclusion is false. There are some goods such that, if there are too many enjoyers, they cease to be enjoyable, just as if a woman has too many lovers she ceases to be lovable.

Goods Incapable of Indefinite Extension

Beauty is one of these goods. There is a definite limit to the number of cars that can gather at Newlands Corner or at Whiteways above Arundel, if Newlands Corner and Whiteways are to be worth visiting. There is a limit to the numbers who at any given moment can climb Great Gable, if Great Gable is to be worth climbing. There is a certain kind of good, solitude in nature, in respect of which this truth is obvious. Indeed, it follows logically from the conception of solitude. In so far, then, as solitude is admitted to be a good—solitude and the partial solitude in which one wanders over the hills or beside the river with a loved woman or an old friend—it follows that to try to increase the amount of this good by quantitative extension is to destroy it.

This obvious truth is increasingly overlooked. Take, for example, a case known to me personally, the case of Midhurst Common, a stretch of grass, heather and pine lying immediately to the west of this uniquely favoured town. This is not the best side of Midhurst ; in fact, it is the worst of the four, but such is the variety of beauty of which Midhurst is the centre, beauty of down and common, of field and hedgerow, of wide-stretching parkland, of river meadow and deep tree-shaded lane, that that which is the worst side of Midhurst would be the best side of almost anywhere else. Alongside Midhurst Common lies "the Severals" where is the best display of rhododendrons known to me anywhere in the country. The Common has also a superb view of the Downs and, except on Boxing Day when the Cowdray Hunt meets there, it is so little frequented that you can pass the day there and not see a person.

Ever since I can remember a horrid brickworks has occupied one corner of the Common. The brickworks was small and comparatively inoffensive and during the slump of the 'thirties almost ceased operations. But with the recent growth of demand for houses and for bricks to build them with there has come a demand for an extension of the brick-works. A controversy accordingly arose as to whether they should be permitted to extend or not. The Manager of the Midhurst Brick and Lime Company argued as follows :—

"The amenities of Midhurst Common," he said, "could not be regarded as important, since so few people enjoyed them." He had, he assured us, "no lack of appreciation of the value of the amenities", but, he added, "my experience is that the Common is not a popularly patronised pleasure resort. I spent the major part of the day there on Good Friday last with the express purpose of testing my previous impression on this point, and I did not encounter more than half a dozen people." It did not occur to the Managing Director that those who wished to preserve Midhurst Common did so precisely because it was a place in which it was still possible not to "encounter more than half a dozen people." It was in fact precisely the fewness of the people that constituted the attraction of the place to the few. If everybody enjoyed the pleasures of Midhurst Common, nobody would enjoy them because there would be no beauty left to enjoy. You cannot appreciate solitude if a multitude is busy appreciating solitude at the same time.

The considerations which I have cited in the case of Midhurst Common have a general applicability. The sense of emptiness and space, for example, which is engendered by a great expanse of marsh stretching away under an evening sky to the sea is a necessary ingredient in one's pleasure in the view from W—. Indeed, many views depend for their significance upon just such a sense. Hence, if many were to enjoy the view from W—., the view would cease to be enjoyable. One takes a wry pleasure in pointing out these obvious things.

2. *A Threnody on Trees.* Or, consider the case of the trees at W—, a long line of elms ranged along the road and now threatened with destruction. The Victorians loved—or said they loved—or said they ought to love—"the highest" when they saw it. We heave a brick at it, especially if it be a tree.

The road along which I walk to the Tube station is lined with a row of noble trees. Last autumn their enemies descended upon them and assaulted them, hewing, hacking and lopping them out of all recognition. Now they stand like a row of corpses in an atrocity picture, holding their mutilated arms in dumb protest to the skies. What is more, I can, for the first time, see the ugly blocks of houses for which they were so merciful a screen.

Every spring, about February, there begins a great pruning and lopping of the London trees. It is ruthlessly, often abominably, done. Granted that for some obscure reason of arboriculture, it is necessary from time to time to cut large pieces from fine trees, some attention might be paid to the shape of the trees selected for treatment, some regard to the amenities of the landscape. No such considerations appear to weigh with the guardians of our London parks and heaths. There is, or rather there was, a particularly fine group of elms on Hampstead Heath, not a hundred yards from my house. They were old trees, shapely and spacious, showing a network of delicate tracery against the winter sky ; today their beauty is gone. Instead, there is a ragged outline of melancholy stumps and lopped limbs jutting bleakly from the outraged trunks.

What, I have wondered, is the reason for this rage against trees ? "Why" I asked one of the mutilators "are you cutting down that elm ? " "Well," he said, "it is getting old and dangerous." This means, I take it, that if one were to stand under it in a high wind or in a thunder storm, it might blow down or perhaps shed a branch or two and that, of course, would be dangerous. But what then ? In a high wind houses often shed tiles and slates from their roofs ; but nobody regards that as a reason for pulling down the houses. And as for thunder storms, anybody who is foolish enough to stand under an old tree in a thunder storm is asking for trouble, and deserves what he gets.

Or again, he said "The tree might fall down and hit a passing motor." But that, surely, would be a most life-preserving action on the tree's part. I do not know how

H

many people are killed by trees in a year—the number, I imagine, is less than a score ; but I do know that in this country alone motors kill between seven and eight thousand and mutilate about two hundred and fifty thousand people a year. Hence any action on the part of trees designed to diminish the number of cars is *ipso facto* an action which will have the effect of increasing the number of people.

Or again, he said "People in the houses or the flats complain that the trees darken their windows" or "obscure their view." In other words, once upon a time somebody went and built his ignoble house or erected his mass-produced block of flats under the shade of a great tree. When the house or the flats were finished, somebody else went to live in them. One day the second somebody looks out of the window or up into the sky and says "Hallo, there is a tree here. It spoils my view ; it must be cut down." It is difficult to resist the temptation of asking the first somebody why he was so foolish as to build his flat or house behind the tree, and the second why he went to live in it.

So much for the trees of town and suburbs. What of country trees ? England needs timber and is too poor to buy all that she needs, so our woods are cut down wholesale and our forest floors defiled by the mud-stained tracks of lorries, caterpillar tractors and bull-dozers. Where once was a cathedral of great trunks soaring a hundred feet or more up to their leafy tops, there is now a wilderness of mutilated stumps, broken boughs and up-turned roots lying higgledy-piggledy on the gashed and wounded earth.

Take a particular case known to me. At the village of S—, in Sussex, there is a vast sprawling mansion set in an estate of many acres which had for years been farmed by a number of tenant farmers. When the expense of the upkeep of the house became too much for the family, it was put up for sale. It was bought by a Syndicate, said to consist of Jews living in London. The Syndicate descended like a blight upon the place, cutting up the estate, selling a little bit here and a little bit there, selling the dairy, selling the garage, selling some of the home farm, selling, in fact, whatever could be made to realise immediate money without regard to the traditions or beauty of the place, and ruthlessly cutting down the trees.

The roads here run between high banks on which grew elms and great oaks. The Syndicate employed a contractor to cut these down, leaving the banks blank and bare. The land hereabouts is studded with little copses, bird-haunted and full of flowers. The Syndicate entered, cut down the big trees and left only bushes, saplings and scrub. In the course of their operations they broke down the fences. Presently the question arose how the tree trunks were to be got away. The only mode of access to the copses lay through farm land and the farmer refused permission to use his land for this purpose. There, then, at the time of writing the great trunks are still lying, while the surface of the land is mauled and gashed by the wheels of the hateful lorries and tractors which have crushed the wood to pieces and left the place looking like a shambles. Pools of water gather in the ruts and in dry weather the broken surface of the earth flies in dust over the surrounding fields.

The scene is typical. Indeed, it might be viewed today almost anywhere in England. Meanwhile, the Jews, who seem to have no feeling for nature, wonder why we dislike them. I suppose that we who care for the English country are only expiating the sins of our ancestors who shut the Jews up in cities for hundreds of years, until nature became for them only raw material for the making of yet more money.

The Conifers

Oh, but you will say, we don't only cut trees down. We plant them as well ; in fact, we never planted so many. And so we do. But what kind of trees do we plant ? The answer is larch and spruce and pines and firs, serried lines of conifers with which we regiment the sweet irregularity of our woodlands. A hundred and fifty years ago the trees of southern England were the oak, the ash, the beech and the elm. To these we looked for our wooden walls, while the pine was the ornamental luxury of the eighteenth century gentleman's garden. In the nineteenth century came a use for pines as pit props, and after "the great war" that ended in Waterloo, the inevitable crowds of unemployed soldiers were set to work to plant them. Meanwhile wooden ships were superseded and the commercial value of the oak and the ash declined. With what result? In England south of the Thames the pines outnumber all the other trees put together, while the oak and the ash bid fair within the next fifty years to subside into the occasional ornaments of gardens and parks.

The Forestry Commission are the chief offenders. In a single year for which the figures are known to me they planted $45\frac{1}{2}$ million softwood trees as compared with three million odd hardwoods. They planted them in regular rows, planted them so closely that nobody could penetrate the thick gloom that broods over the wood, even if anybody were to wish to do so. The only way to enter one of these modern conifer woods is to walk along the alley ways that run between them. You can no longer wander at will, you can see no view, you hear no birds, and presently the oppression of your spirit becomes as deadening as the constriction of your vision.

But just in case you still don't know what is the matter with pines, I append a list of their main defects :—

(a) There is no bird life in a pine wood ; indeed, their chief inhabitants are insects. Even poor Hudson, when he was sent to live among the pines because of his weak chest, could only find ants to write about.

(b) There are neither undergrowth nor flowers.

(c) A pine wood does not visibly change with the seasons, but is always of the same dreary dullness.

All over England the softwoods are ousting the hard. I think of the most distinctively English place that I know, know best and because it *is* distinctively English, love most, which is, once again, the country round Midhurst and more particularly the country to the south of Midhurst. Here is fully displayed every beauty that can grace the southern

English scene. To the south is the line of the Downs ; the foothills and the plain are dotted with little copses which in spring are alive with primroses and daffodils and threaded with fast-running streams. There are agreeable villages and there are green meadows studded with great trees. These last are outstanding. Nowhere are there oaks more sturdy or beeches more gracious. There are great elms, in some ways the loveliest of them all, standing silent and solitary in the fields, and an occasional poplar, like an exclamation mark, comments enigmatically upon the beauty of the scene. . . . Is such beauty, one wonders, quite meaningless, or is it perhaps the window through which one can obtain a glimpse of the reality that lies beyond ? Alas, we shall never know, for ours is the last generation privileged to have intercourse with unspoiled, natural beauty. In fifty years' time oaks, beeches, elms and poplars will have gone. For what inducement will there be to keep them ? They are hopelessly uneconomical ; they take long to mature and there is no profit in them. So out upon them and down with them and let the English country become a paradise of Sitka spruces and Douglas firs, and look for all the world like Canada or Norway or Russia. . . .

The Downs

The substitution of softwoods and houses for noble trees is only one of the innumerable ways in which the beauty of England is destroyed. Take, for example, the Sussex Downs. We used to think of them in terms of larks, lambs and dew ponds. Today one's dominant impression is all too often of half dismantled radar camps, trailing strands of barbed wire, lengths of rusting railway track and crumbling concrete. From one end of the Downs to the other, from the cement works at Itford to the quarrying at Duncton, from the closing of the rights of way on Chanctonbury to the burning of the old yews on Bow Hill, from the erection of concrete posts and wire fencing at Stanmer to the destruction of the beeches at Winton Street in the Cuckmere Valley, from the Air Ministry's Radar Station at Beachy Head to the closing of the bridle road that runs from Clayton to Lewes, the tale of destruction and vulgarisation runs. Our generation cannot create beauty for itself ; it can only destroy the beauty that has come down to it. By so doing it bequeaths a poorer and thinner life to its posterity. Our children may be cleverer, more knowledgeable, even more virtuous than ourselves ; it seems certain that they will have invented methods of destruction both of man and nature whose power and ingenuity will make us look like the veriest tyros in the art. But as things are going, it is hard to avoid the conclusion that the knowledge of and pleasure in nature, both tamed and wild, which our generation still in its measure possesses and enjoys, will be privileges denied to our grandchildren. If that were to happen, as it bids fair to do, their lives will lack at least one element of value which all our predecessors have known and of which even we, starved of beauty as we are, can still intermittently avail ourselves.

The Pleasure of Cassandra

What relevance, it may be asked, has this lament on the destruction of trees to the pleasures of the self, for it is grief and indignation rather than pleasure that have inspired the writing of the last few pages ? There are three answers. First, there is the pleasure of Cassandra. I derive, I must admit, a very considerable enjoyment from prophesying woe, when the woe is of our own making and could, therefore, be avoided. I like to point to a roadside elm or to a great oak standing solitary and solid in its field, and say "What a lovely old tree ! Why don't they cut it down ? " I love to comment, as I have commented above, on some proposal to cut down a row of noble trees and substitute a row of Council cottages in their place, "We can't create beauty for ourselves. We might at least try to preserve the beauty that has come down to us." I love, in a word, to look forward, as I have just done, to a southern England which has become a single, vast suburb sprawling from London to the coast, studded with a number of carefully spaced preserved beauty spots, inhabited by Government-hired rustics complete with smock frocks, gnarled sticks, horny hands and old-time accents. My state of mind, as I make my bitter comments, putting my own nose in the muck and rubbing other people's noses in it, combines the pleasures of the masochist and of the sadist. Moreover, I tell myself that it is just possible that I may goad my hearers into feeling a sense of shame ; just possible, but extremely unlikely.

Secondly, there is the pleasure of official-bamboozling and official-baiting. I have at various times taken my share in the thankless task of countryside preservation. As a member of The Friends of the Lake District, I have sought—how unsuccessfully—to protect the solitudes of the Lakeland valleys. As an officer of The Ramblers' Association, I have fought for the access of the rambler to wild places irrespective of the rights of sportsmen, the depredations of water undertakings and the claims of hydro-electric schemes.

Now I have discovered that a simple appeal to the value of beauty or of solitude is of no avail. A local authority may prate of the beauty and the antiquity of the locality ; a leader writer, a government official or the executive of a business undertaking, may pay lip service to the values of solitude and wildness ; but when it comes to profit or convenience, to the siting of factories, the location of industry, the construction of reservoirs or the building of houses, all such considerations are immediately brushed aside. Hence the only recourse left to the would-be beauty preserver is to meet the enemy with his own weapons, to oppose profit with profit, to confront convenience with convenience. And so I have acquired a horrid ingenuity in the devising of good, practical, hard-headed, common-sensible man of the world arguments in favour of not doing the things that the enemy proposes to do.

We are accustomed to the rationalisation of evil to make it appear other than the thing it is ; but there are also rationalisations of good, since good unrationalised is of no account. And so we have to speak to the would-be destroyers and uglifiers in their own language, saying, for example, that the Lakeland firs and pines are bad for the Herdwick sheep, or that the proposed cement works in the Peak will be inaccessible and the transport of their products excessively expensive, or that the great sums spent on machinery for opencast coal mining (£7,000,000 in dollars in 1946 alone) could have been better spent in mechanising pits crying out for modern methods, or that the hydro-electric schemes for harnessing the waters of Scottish lochs will not employ as many people as their promoters anticipate and that they will not be local people. In the matter of the Snowdon hydro-electric scheme, for example, nothing could exceed the forthrightness of our denial that we seek by the with-holding of electricity to perpetuate the age of lamps and candles. But what we also deny is that the destruction of Snowdon's wildness and solitude will be the best way of providing the electricity, and so we invoke friendly tech-nicians to demonstrate that a single thermal power station for the whole of Wales which could be built in four, or at most five, years could produce as much electricity as all the piece-meal hydro-electric schemes proposed for Wales, of which Snowdon's is one, which would take at least twenty years to complete. But what we dare not say is that the Snowdon hydro-electric scheme will, for the sake of speeding up by a few years the removal of inconveniences that people have tolerated for centuries, sacrifice irreplaceable natural splendours for ever.

Now the pleasure of inventing these solid-seeming, horse-sense, utilitarian arguments is at bottom nothing but my old pleasure of official-bamboozling and baiting dressed up in virtuous guise. And this, as I have already explained, is a highly peculiar and personal pleasure, a pleasure of the self.

There are, thirdly, the pleasures of just indignation. It is good, says Plato, to be indignant about the things that are proper for indignation. Now most of my indignation proceeds from trifling or unworthy causes. I am indignant with women for neglecting their kitchens, with boys for making noises, with officials for sending inappropriate forms or for sending forms at all, with the countryman or estate agent who says "It's only a mile off" when in fact it is two, with the motor mechanic who, when the beastly engine won't start, says "It *should* do", with the travel agency for booking me a seat directly over the wheels of the carriage, with the railway company because the train is late or with myself because it is punctual and I miss it.

Now these many causes of irritation and indignation testify to nothing but that I am grown into an irritable, testy old man. But every now and then I feel an indignation which I know to be worthy and rejoice to feel it, being proud of myself because I am still capable of feeling it. Such is the indignation that I feel for physical cruelty, at the sight of a wild bird in a cage or of a dog permanently chained up. Timid as I naturally am and anxious for a quiet life, I show a surprising amount of courage in bearding fierce and brutal persons—for example, the horrible women who keep linnets and nightingales in cages till they sing their poor little hearts out, or dogs on chains until they bark themselves mad.

Now one of the things that arouses my just indignation is man's indifference to natural beauty and in particular his hatred of trees. A man was cutting down the elm tree which stood at the cross roads. It had elm disease, he said, was dangerous and must be cut down. I used my argument about falling trees saving life by falling on motorists, but he didn't see the point and thought I was being funny. He then proposed to cut down the elm in my own garden. It would, he said, have to come down sooner or later, for it, too, was diseased and it might as well come down sooner as later. If, he said, it were to fall across the road I should be liable for the obstruction that it caused and its removal would cost me a pretty penny. As he was there he would, he said, cut it down for me cheaply. He was very earnest with me to let him do this thing.

I felt myself getting very angry, told myself that this was a worthy and justified anger, took pleasure in it and deliberately let myself rip. How rarely it is that you can enjoy the pleasure of telling a man what you think of him, that he is a man of tin and brass, begotten in a loud speaker and born in the entrails of a car, that he got his mother's milk from a petrol pump on the Kingston by-pass, that he is losing any semblance of humanity that his ancestors may have possessed and is already more than half way along the road that leads from man to the insect, and that even if I knew that the tree would fall on him, I still wouldn't have it cut down. He didn't understand much of what I said but, goodness, how I enjoyed saying it.

CHAPTER VIII

The Pleasures (?) of Age

The Beastliness of Age

Almost, I am tempted to say, there aren't any. And I take a wry personal pleasure in convincing myself that there aren't and in saying so. All round me my contemporaries are trumpeting the virtues of age. "I have never," one says "enjoyed myself so much as I do now." "It is only now," says another "that I am learning how to live." "I am only just beginning," says a third "to find out what are the things I really like doing, the things that are really worth while, and to insist on doing them." That last asseveration has a ring of truth—I can well believe that all his life, poor chap, he has been trying to like and to enjoy the things that public opinion insisted that he ought to like and to enjoy, or (worse) persuaded himself that he did in fact like and enjoy them—and might well have been echoed by me, if there were anything that I now really liked doing.

As for the rest—cant and fiddlesticks ! With what pleasure I adapt for the benefit of these hypocritically hearty old men Dr. Johnson's remark about poverty. "Sir," I say to them in effect, "all the arguments which you adduce to show that growing old is not an evil show it, in fact, to be a very great evil. Nobody strives to convince you that you can have a good time when you are full of health and vigour."

Samuel Butler made a similar point after his manner when he declared, "Of course I hate growing old ; but, you see, it is the only way I have yet discovered of living a long life."

And of course one hates it ; hates every year and every minute of it. I have hated it ever since a young man ran down a hill faster than I could. At once I began to prate of growing old—I was thirty-five at the time—and kept it up continuously for years hoping that, if I made a sufficient fuss about being old when I was quite palpably in the prime of life, I should provoke everybody into indignant denials, and so put·off the evil day when they would say to one another : "Joad's getting old ; he is breaking up." Now that I really am old, I largely abstain from mentioning it.

I am disposed, then, to agree with the view which John Stuart Mill attributes to his father in that fascinating Autobiography of his, surely the best in the language : "He thought human life a poor thing at best after the freshness of youth and of unsatisfied curiosity had gone by." And what a weight of authority is on Mill's side.

Some Authorities

For example, there is Sophocles's "Not to be born is past all praying best. Easily the next best is to return as soon as possible whence we came." Or Bacon's "What, then, remains but that we still should cry not to be born, or, being born, to die ? " Or Winwood Read's "Life is one long tragedy ; creation is one great crime." Or Bernard Shaw's "every man over forty is a scoundrel." Or Chesterfield's "Statesmen and beauties are very rarely sensible of the gradations of their decay ; and, too sanguinely hoping to shine on in their meridian, often set with contempt and ridicule," or his "The heart never grows better by age ; I fear rather worse, always harder."

And then there is that terrible last chapter of Ecclesiastes known to us all from readings in the College chapel from our youth up, because of the lovely sound of the words— "Or ever the silver cord be loosed, or the golden bowl be broken, or the pitcher be broken at the fountain. . . . Then shall the dust return to the earth as it was : and the spirit shall return unto God who gave it. Vanity of vanities, saith the preacher, all is vanity,"—sonorities, whose beauty could not wholly fail of its entrance even into our Philistine ears, though none of us, I suppose, had the faintest idea what they meant. Though "of making many books there is no end" we must have clearly understood even then, and to "much study is a weariness of the flesh" we vigorously assented.

It was only later in life, when I was complaining about the length of time it took me to get well when anything went wrong with me, and how I never seemed to get *completely* well, that a wise man pointed out that the whole chapter was an allegorical description of the distressing characteristics of age. He proceeded to expound. For example, that disconcerting feature to which I have just referred—namely, that when you have been ill you never seem to get wholly well again, or are no sooner well of one thing than you are ill of another, the failing body going bad on you somewhere else—how perfectly it is touched off by "The clouds return after the rain." Some of the references are plain enough. "The keepers of the house," presumably, the hands, "shall tremble." "The grinders cease because they are few". "Those that look out of the windows be darkened" and so on. And what about "And he shall rise up at the voice of the bird" as touching that annoying habit of the old man, of waking up very early in the morning, so that just as his time becomes diminishingly worth spending, his life diminishingly worth living, there turns out to be more to spend and live ? Others, such as "the almond tree shall flourish" are baffling—unless in the east almond blossom is white. And why should "the grasshopper be a burden ? " Does it mean merely that old men are incapable of carrying weights or bearing burdens ?

But the general picture is clear enough. It isn't much fun being old, and so I have found it.

Energy and Variety

Looking back over my life, I can see how much of its happiness, such as it was—and for twenty-five years or so it was, I think, a decidedly happier life than that of most—was due to a superabundance of energy and vitality. This expressed itself not only, though it did primarily, in the things of the body, but in a versatility of activities, interests and pursuits which enabled me to turn with ease and rapidity from the things of the body to those of the mind and even of the spirit, and so imparted to my life that variety with which its happiness was so intimately bound up.

I have played games, football, tennis and hockey. I spent most of my holidays among mountains and at one time as a member of the famous Trevelyan manhunt, used to run, Whitsun after Whitsun, up and down the slopes of the Lakeland hills. I went long cross-country walks at all times, and presently I became a keen, though far from expert rider.

I passed from these physical activities to others of a different order with ease and despatch. I would get up early and walk for two hours or more in the country and be at my desk in London by 11.30. I would go hunting in the morning and return to attend a committee meeting in the afternoon. I would go for an all-day walk alone on a Saturday and turn up at a country house at tea time tired out and muddy for a social weekend. From my talents as a quick-change artist in this matter of activities and enjoyments I derived an acute personal pleasure, a pleasure, I fear, not unmixed with feelings of superiority. How I would look down my nose at the overclad men and fat women I met at tea in the weekend country house, as I thought of their lackadaisical drive down in the gloomy car, of their large luncheon and of the indigestion that succeeded it. As I looked round upon the white faces of my fellow committee members, I would ask myself what they knew of walking the ridge of the Downs at 8 a.m. in hot sunlight while all the valley below was seething and swirling in a sea of mist. They had just come up, hadn't they, from their suburban hutches by the 8.55 or burrowed ill-temperedly in the earth and emerged at last in the sunlight packed like sardines and blinking like moles? As I consorted with the powerful and the important, the witty and the smart, at reception, party or club, I would remind myself of the uncouth, silent chaps, the hearty, stupid girls, so kindly and so *gauche*, with whom only a few hours before I had been walking across the fields or through the woods of Surrey on a cross-country ramble.

It was at summer schools that these rapid changes of activity, scene and pursuit achieved their fullest realisation. Alone among the lecturers I had been on the all-day ramble, had, indeed, led it. Of all that group of keen, political debaters, I alone had played in the cricket match. I alone among the organisers, the leaders and the *élite* generally knew the dimmer rank and file—had I not swum and walked with them, beaten that timid young man on the tennis court, made love to that pretty young thing ?

In sum, I was enabled by reason of this versatility of activity not only to enjoy a more varied life than that of most, but to cultivate a greater variety of human contacts. I believe that I knew far more different sorts of people than it is given to most people to know, and my life was in proportion richer and more coloured than the average.

In retrospect I can see how completely this life of varied activities and rapid, easy transitions was dependent on overflowing energy. If I liken myself to others who, from a similar abundance of energy, specialised in a similar quickness of change from the mental to the physical and back again—to Trollope writing for three hours at his novel and then to a day's work at his Civil Service desk, or getting up early in London to hunt all day in the country and then back again to London to write in the evening ; or to Dickens who, after a morning at his writing, would go for a twelve or even a twenty mile walk, preparatory to finishing the day by taking a leading part in the production of the play which he had written and organised himself, and if I point out that the outstanding characteristic of these great men was also an abounding energy, I hope that I shall not be thought to liken myself to them in any other respect.

The Energetic Man in Old Age

But the energetic man grows old badly. For to what is he to turn when his energy fails ? All those pursuits and activities upon which he has been used to rely, I will not say for his happiness, but for the not having enough breathing space to have time to wonder whether he was happy or not— and that is the best negative recipe for happiness that life has taught me—become as the years pass more arduous and exhausting. Increasingly, they come to be felt as a burden. Presently the burden becomes too great to be borne, and with mingled relief and regret it is dropped.

And what then ? The life of the once energetic man is emptied of most of what has hitherto given it meaning and distinction. He is like the professional beauty at fifty or the athlete fattening into late middle age.

In my own case every phase of relinquishment was observed with dismay, every step of retreat taken with regret. It was with consternation that one noticed oneself first giving up singles at tennis and then tiring after four sets of doubles ; or dreading instead of welcoming one's service game. The twenty miles walk dwindled to ten and then to five or six, interspersed with frequent halts and comforted by an ever more elaborately packed lunch. Instead of running after other men up and down the slopes of half a dozen different Lakeland heights from Brandreth down into Ennerdale, then up Great Gable, then down again to Ennerdale and so on to the Haystacks, one climbed once only and that with ever-increasing labour. After three hours in the saddle I would grow tired and want to come home.

As for the pleasures of love, they faded and staled with each successive year. When I was a young man, I looked forward to the day when I should be free from the tyranny of desire. Into what humiliating circumstances it had led me ; through what wastes of boredom it had dragged me, only too often to encounter frustration at the end. I was a whole-hearted adherent of the "expense of spirit in a waste of shame" view of love, or, more precisely, love oscillated for me between that and an enfeebling sentimentalism. Yet I could by no means win free of it ; it was as if, every now and then, one had had to get up from one's desk and swat a mosquito that was buzzing in the room in which one was trying to write. But now that emancipation has come, or almost come, how wistfully one yearns for the galling of those enchanting chains. Moreover, others have come to take their place, as I shall tell later in this chapter. The pleasures of food and drink remain ; indeed, they grow, but increasing weight forbids some ; occasional illness denies others.

To cease to take the lead in physical pursuits was to cease to exercise a number of carefully cultivated skills and talents, with the result that one's personality shrank with the contraction of the channels of its expression, and the variety of one's acquaintance diminished with that of one's pursuits.

What "They" Say

"Quite so" they say, "No doubt" and "Very well." Also, "What else do you expect ? " and "Why not, pray ? As you grow older it is only natural to draw in your horns, and the process is far from being all loss. All your life you have been so busy thinking you have had no time to stop and think ; so busy saving time that you have had no time to spare ; so busy talking that you have had no time to listen. Now you will be able to listen. You may hear something, something that you have never heard before, the music it may be of the spheres, or perhaps the still small voice of God. Even if it is only the beating of your own heart that you hear, it is high time that you paid a little attention to yourself ; acquired, in fact, self-knowledge." "Also", they say, "you will now be able to sit back and watch life ; in particular to watch over and participate in the lives of the young. Old people get their greatest pleasure through living in the lives of others."

Solitude of the Old

Some self-knowledge perhaps I may have acquired, but I would much sooner be without it. Whenever during my life I have had leisure to look within, I have felt so afraid of what I found there that I have looked outward again as hurriedly

I

as I could. All the many activities and varied interests of my life are seen in retrospect to be no more than a series of devices for fixing my gaze determinedly outward. The Greeks, I am aware, recommended self-knowledge, and so do those who laud the life of the old. But whether self-knowledge is a good thing or not depends, surely, on the nature of that which is known. If the self is nice to know, the more one knows of it the better. But if not, not. Why, after all, should one fix one's attention on unworthy objects ?

Similarly with self-consciousness. One of the accompaniments of the life of the ageing man is increasing solitude. When one is a schoolboy, one lives in a herd. Even as a young man, one goes about in gangs ; you go out walking all day with anything up to a score of people and sleep in a dormitory at hostel or summer school with half a dozen others. You enjoy such a rich variety of acquaintanceships that it is not surprising if a few, a very few, should crystallise into friendships. And there are always the women whom one has loved. . . .

In middle-age the gangs of companions have disappeared and their place has been taken by the hundreds of meaningless contacts that business, politics or the professions bring. You never saw so many people who meant so little to you ; of the friends only two or three remain.

But by the time that old age is reached even the two or three have dropped off. Some are dead, others have gone away, others, again, are submerged beneath the waters of their family lives. Realising that you will never replace them, since you are incapable of making new friends, you cling to them as long as you can, but the dynamism of the friendship has evaporated with its enjoyment. Old men are apt to be moody, surly and cross grained. The antennæ with which they have felt the world are being withdrawn and increasingly they are shut up within themselves. Consequently their interest in and for one another diminishes. Presently you realise that you are living not on the income but on the capital of your friendships, and in course of time even this is exhausted.

The old, then, lead solitary lives and increasingly hold communion with the selves upon which they are thrown back. But whether this is a good thing or a bad depends upon whether one's self is a nice person to commune with. I venture to repeat the point, since it seems to be taken for granted that the increasing opportunities for self-knowledge, self-study, self-consciousness and self-communion that old age offers are a something gained. I can only put it on record that I would much sooner be without them, especially now that I am old. Indeed, I was an infinitely more interesting person to be with thirty years ago when my personality was enriched by a dozen interests and fertilised by a hundred contacts, than I am today when my soul, hardened and narrowed by an increasing egotism, has lost interest even as an object of contemplation.

Living in the Lives of Others

Oh yes, and before I forget it, there is that business of living in the lives of others. What a horrible thing to do, even if one were capable of it. Who am I, that I should peer into, spy upon, oversee, supervise, watch over the lives of the young ? Interfering impertinence ! Infernal cheek ! I am sure that nothing would please the young less than the knowledge that some doting old fool was taking an interest in them ; apart altogether from the fact that most old fools aren't doting at all but censorious. Most of those who have reached my time of life, in spite of their alleged contentment with the condition of age, can never quite forgive the young for their robust enjoyment of the pleasures that they, the old, must forgo. The young have two good eyes to see with, two good ears to hear with, two good legs to walk and climb and play games with. Above all the young can make love and do. As one observes them, all one's boasted freedoms turn out to be so many sour grapes ; for in one's heart one envies them and grudges them the pleasures denied to oneself. "How those young people do go on" one says to oneself, "Really it ought to be stopped."

We become adepts at the most elaborate forms of "sour

grapes" rationalisation. Old men give young men good advice when they can no longer give them bad examples, and old women still make play with the fading figure of Mrs. Grundy to deter their juniors from the pleasures denied to themselves by lack of charm. And if the juniors get found out, the old women can still take it out of them to some purpose and turn their lives into a little hell of blaming and scolding and scorning. How they resent the invention of birth control which makes it so easy for their juniors not to get found out !

No, the interest which the old take in the lives of the young is very far from being disinterested. I know few young people who would not much sooner be without it. As for the business of joying with their joys and sorrowing with their sorrows and so on, it is for most of us inhibited by that ever-hardening shell of narrowing interest and increasing egotism by which, as I have pointed out, the old endeavour to protect themselves against the aggressions and invasions of the oncoming young. (Yes, I know I attributed the egotism and the rest to myself, but I don't really believe that my contemporaries are much better.) Besides, how can we expect to go on being interested in those platitudinous pleasures and triumphs of the young, those commonplace sorrows ? We have been through them all ourselves, and to experience them again is like turning over the pages of an old love-letter or reading once again the book that we have outgrown.

Alleged Compensations

What equivalent gains have come to take the place of the lost pleasures of the body and the lost pleasures of variety ? With meditation and recollection in solitude I have already dealt. All very well, I have concluded, if, being a nice person, you are a good companion for your solitude and a pleasant object to meditate upon, with a nice, bright, creditable life to recollect. But neither I nor my life satisfy these conditions. Meditation should, I suppose, be rightly directed upon the universal consciousness, upon the spirit which is behind things or—not to put too fine a point upon it—upon God. But, though I believe in Him, I don't know how to meditate upon Him. Still less do I know how to make contact with Him.

The Life of the Mind

Ideas, controversy, discussing, reading—in a word, the activities of the mind ? These still go on, but they are not what they were. When I was young, I had a passion for ideas. All the philosophical heresies, hedonism, solipsism, egoism, came to me with a fine and seductive freshness, with a bloom on their heretical cheeks. I picked them up, made them mine, revelled in them, and trotted them out for the discomfiture of all comers. The discussions and controversies that ensued, as when I demonstrated to a respectable self-sacrificing uncle that in the last resort he did everything in order to obtain pleasure for himself and that he was no more unselfish than I was, were meat and drink to me.

But now these delightful heresies are used and stale, and no new ones have arisen to take their place. Moreover, do I not have to write and teach them to get my living ? And why should I do gratis, merely for the pleasure of shocking, what it is my business to do for pay ? Besides, I am not now sufficiently interested in people to derive pleasure from shocking them.

I have long ago renounced the hope that philosophical writing or discussion will reveal truth. In fact, I am sufficiently infected (privately, though not professionally) with the Logical Positivist mode of thinking, fashionable in my time, to doubt whether such a thing as philosophical truth exists, or if it does, whether it is attainable.

At any rate I do not believe that the world of thought holds any new ideas for me and shall, therefore, never again enjoy the thrill of meeting them for the first time. By this I mean that I already know, not so much all the ideas that there are to know, as all those that my increasingly rigid mind is capable of taking in. If there are any new ones that I don't know about, my mind, I feel pretty sure, would be

133

closed to them. Thus I am unable to make head or tail of Existentialism and Personalism which are to me high-sounding names for pretentious, cosmic flapdoodle, and I have been dead to new movements in poetry, new schools of painting and new musical forms these twenty-five years past. Thus I derive little or no pleasure, from the poems of T. S. Eliot, the paintings of Picasso or the music of Prokovief, Shostakovich or Britten.

That Ideas Cannot Change the World

I once had a passion for ideas in another sense. Through them, I believed, you could change the world. I never doubted that men were reasonable in the sense that if something was true or right or just, and if you could show them that it was, arguing with them in season and out of season and never desisting from the accumulation of facts with which to support your arguments and from the demon-stration of the conclusions to which they inescapably led, in the end you could persuade their reasons and so form their convictions. I agreed in fact with what John Stuart Mill tells us about his father—"So complete was my father's reliance on the influence of reason over the minds of mankind, whenever it is allowed to reach them, that he felt as if all would be gained if the whole population were taught to read, if all sorts of opinions were allowed to be addressed to them by word and in writing, and if by means of a suffrage they could nominate a legislature to give effect to the opinions they adopted." In other words, as a man thinks, so will he act. Hence, to persuade thought is to determine conduct and ideas can change the world.

I shall never forget the thrill with which in the light of this belief I first read Shaw and Wells. Their ideas went to my head like wine. Indeed, into the whole movement of liberation and revolt of the pre-1914 period of which the negative aspect was the disruption of Victorianism and the positive, the advocacy of Socialism, I threw myself with a passion of intellectual abandon and delight.

Nor was it only Shaw and Wells who produced this heady

effect but in a less degree Galsworthy, Bennett and Granville Barker and, later, Chesterton and Belloc. All these I read in a glow of enthusiasm which is unlike anything I have felt for literature since. They liberated and expanded my mind, opening up for me a new world of ideas. Social evils could be diminished, economic injustice abolished, poverty alleviated and society moulded nearer to the heart's desire by dint of hard reasoning and argumentative effort supported by goodwill.

This juvenile optimism could not, of course, be expected to continue, and the time came when I reluctantly taught myself to abandon my belief that even the writings of Shaw and Wells could alter men's habits. The change was in part the consequence of my infection by the intellectual corruption of the times in which I lived. I was unable wholly to resist that scepticism in regard to reason which has eaten like an acid into the thought of our age. I could denounce in theory, but could not wholly escape in practice the infection of the psycho-analysts' fashionable demonstration of the alarming extent to which the working of the rational consciousness were determined by currents of unreason which ran below the surface. Nor was I wholly unmoved by the Marxist contention that our beliefs, so far at any rate as morals and politics are concerned, were an expression of the social and economic class to which we belonged. It was a man's class position that was reflected in, the interests of his class that were promoted by the arguments he adopted and the conclusions he came to.

But what in the end mattered more than either psychological or economic theories was the lamentable absence of visible improvement. Shaw and Wells won a complete victory in the intellectual field, and the world has gone from bad to worse ever since. With the doubtful exception of the economic position of the working classes in this country and in America, in respect of justice, humanity, tolerance, freedom, kindliness, consideration for others, not to speak of graciousness of manners and amenity of life, in respect, in a word, of civilisation, the world today is manifestly on a lower plane than it was in 1914, when the movements of the mind and the spirit with which I was identified were apparently advancing all along the line. On the debit side intolerance, obscurantism and fanaticism, expressing themselves in the grossest tyranny and injustice, with their inevitable accompaniments of secret police, arbitrary arrest, imprisonment without trial and the agony of gross physical torture, evils from which the world in which I grew up was comparatively free, are once again rampant.

My disillusion in regard to the power of ideas received its most notable confirmation from war. Throughout my adult life I have been a pacifist, never doubting that war was the ultimate evil and believing, therefore, that nothing that could happen to a people as the result of not going to war could be so disastrous as war itself. I believed that this conclusion could be demonstrated by irrefragable arguments and that the propositions that war never paid, that not only were none of the goods that it purported to achieve in fact achieved, but that evils which nobody had foreseen inevitably accrued, had only to be stated to carry immediate conviction. Besides, nobody wanted war, at least none of the people that I met wanted war. To the man and woman in the street war could bring nothing but "taxes, widows and wooden legs," that is to say, nothing but suffering, heartache and loss. Hence, it was only because men were bemused by propaganda that they were willing to fight in wars. Dispel the propaganda by stating the case against war and the "idea," which, I did not doubt, embodied the truth, would prevail. So, at least, I had taught myself to believe. After an unremitting advocacy of pacifism lasting for twenty years I still believe in the "idea" but not that it will prevail ; for with what heart can a man of my generation who has lived through two wars and sees a third visibly approaching put his trust in the efficacy of ideas to ward off disaster and promote good ? No, the reforming zeal engendered by belief in the efficacy of ideas has gone and been replaced by the common-place disillusion of the old.

136

Old Man's Lament on the Decline of Literature

What of the vaunted pleasures of literature ? Of old men's reading I shall say something in a moment. Here it is relevant to point to the obvious fact that the great men of my nonage have had no successors. Hardy, Meredith, Henry James and Max Beerbohm, Shaw, Wells, Bennett, Galsworthy, Chesterton, Belloc, Conrad, A. E. Housman and, a little later the gods of the early 'twenties, Aldous Huxley, E. M. Forster, Virginia Woolf, D. H. Lawrence— who is there to set beside them ? When I was growing up there were at any given moment half a dozen writers whose books, as they came out, one could count upon every-body having read, or at least thinking it worth while to pretend that they had read. As a result there was a common background of literary information upon which standards could be built, by which taste could be formed and from which criticism could spring. Thus, talk about books took place within a context of knowledge and enjoyment in which most of us shared. Today there is no equivalent context. For what standard authors are there whom all read as a matter of course ? T. S. Eliot ? Possibly. Graham Greene ? Perhaps. Somerset Maugham ? Certainly. But Eliot is not everybody's cup of tea. Graham Greene is to my mind vastly over-rated, and we have all said and read what there is to say and read about Maugham long ago.

No, reading and discussing the books one reads are not the fun they were.

The Waning of Love and Friendship

What other joys of the mind or of the spirit have come to take the place of that zest in physical activity and energetic variety that have passed away ? The pleasures of love and friendship ? But one can no longer make love and what possibility of friendship is there with a woman from which the element of sex is lacking ? Once I would have said none ; now I am not so sure. But of that, too, I will speak when this lament is done.

As to friendship, consider the old. There they are in

clubs, pensions, boarding-houses, hotels, hospitals and poor law institutions. Do they love each other? Emphatically they do not. From time to time a couple of old cronies can be seen sitting together by the fireside or in the sunlight, bragging of past glories, but they are so unrepresentative as to call for comment. For the most part, the old, when thrown into one another's company, spend their time in hating, thwarting and spiting one another. They make charges against one another, complaining how this one or that takes more than his or her fair share of food or air or space or light ; or they accuse one another of usurping privileges to which they are not entitled. They form cliques and gangs against one another. They give one another black looks as they meet. Many are not even on speaking terms. No, the old are not remarkable for the pleasure that they take in one another's company. Nor from these generalisations can I exclude myself. In place of the score of friends that I once possessed I have now but two or three. Nor, I think, do they like me as much as they once did, or I them. We go on meeting one another, as the old do, out of habit, and perhaps we cling together a little more than we did, being only too conscious of our inability to attract or be attracted by anyone else.

Of pain and the wearing out of the body that is like a rotten old boat, which when you patch it up in one place springs a leak somewhere else—of these things I say nothing. That they darken and cloud the life of the old is obvious. They also narrow it, so that the mind that has ranged through the universe to map the stars or unlock the secrets of the atom is contracted to the confines of an aching tooth ; the spirit that has refined itself in contact with beauty, or lifted itself to commune with God is brought down to the level of a stammering bladder. But these things are too well-known to call for comment. Even those who prize old age or strive to make the old contented, commend it in spite of and not because of them. Nor do I believe that pain and illness make people nicer ; on the contrary, they make them irritable and egotistical.

The Credit Side

What entries are there on the credit side ? They fall into two classes. First, there are those investments which pay increasing dividends as one grows older. In my case there are three, music, chess and nature or, rather, work in nature, by which I mean that, though my pleasure in trees or flowers or views or lakes or mountains or sunsets is static or even diminishes, my pleasure in doing things with my hands, in gardening, making an asparagus bed, planting bulbs and trees, making bonfires, scattering seed, distributing dung, making hay, building a rick, picking up sugar beet, slicing sugar beet tops—my pleasure even in that dreariest of all farming operations, hoeing, continually grows. But of none of these things will I speak since their consolatory character has been often remarked upon, precisely because the pleasure in them is common and not private or personal. Besides, of music I speak elsewhere, while of the processes of nature and of the pleasures of work in and with nature, what is there to say that has not been said dozens of times far better than I could hope to say it ?

Let me, then, come to those compensating pleasures such as they are—and Heaven forbid that I should make much of them—which are the peculiar and private pleasures of my ageing self.

THE PLEASURES OF AGE

Literary Struldbrugs

First, then, as to reading. My pleasure in reading has, as I have explained, on the whole, declined, but there is one counter-balancing factor. I now read what I want to read. Let me explain.

During most of my life I have been browbeaten by authority, or persuaded by friends or spurred on by my own desire to keep up with the times and not be left out of the swim, or impelled by a sense of literary shame—I simply couldn't abide the thought that I was lacking in sensibility and unable to appreciate what I was assured on good

authority was important, significant, fresh or original ;
I wanted to keep myself ready and prepared like a wise
virgin to welcome beauty or originality in whatever strange
or unexpected guise they might present themselves—into
spending a great deal of time in reading works which I did
not really enjoy. Good taste, I had early been taught,
"does not come by chance or nature." "It is," as Sir
Joshua Reynolds says, "a long and laborious business to
acquire it."   I knew, too, that beauty is often difficult
of access. It is fashioned by the artist out of the chaos
of the world in the torment of his soul, and it may well
be that it cannot be fully enjoyed except by those who in
their own lives have known something of his struggle and
pain. All this I knew or, at least, suspected and was prepared, therefore, provided that a writer was presented to me
with the backing of a sufficient reputation, to take him on
trust and to persevere. Where my pleasure or interest were
doubtful, I gave him the benefit of the doubt. I remembered
the difficulty I had in making my way through the preliminary thickets of introduction and explanation that
guard the works of Scott and Dickens, and how I had enjoyed them afterwards and been glad that I had persevered.

The writers that I have approached in this reverent
spirit fall into two classes. First there were the great
classics. The corridors of literary history are piled high with
books that have come down to us with reputations which,
as it seems to me, are out of all proportion to their merits.
They are like literary Struldbrugs which go on from age to
age, respected by all but read by few and enjoyed by none.
Take Goethe for instance. I am one of the few who have
read the whole of *Wilhelm Meister*, the dullest great book in
the world. I have also toiled through *The Conversations with
Eckermann*. I have broken my teeth upon the dimmer
Scott's—*The Fortunes of Nigel* and *Peveril of the Peak,* for
example—and loyally read through—an act of piety if
ever there was one—those dreadful early Hardy's. (Did
ever a great man write worse books than *The Hand of
Ethelberta* and *The Laodicean* ?) I have read long and hard

140

in *The Anatomy of Melancholy*. I have done my best to read Smollett, and once persuaded myself that I liked *Tristram Shandy*, but then I was very young and looking back can see this to have been a clear case of being hypnotised by a reputation.

Pushkin and Gogol, Victor Hugo and Stendthal, even Zola —all these I have done my best with, but the best didn't amount to very much. As a professional duty but not as a pleasure, I have read among the heavier, *St. Augustine* and *St. Thomas,* and among the lighter philosophers and wits Gratian's *The Art of Worldly Wisdom*, Lord Chesterfield and la Rochefoucauld. But of the "heavies" Plato is the only one that I read with pleasure as well as profit, and as to the "lights," Samuel Butler's *Notebooks* seem to me to be worth all Goethe and la Rochefoucauld and Chesterfield and Montaigne—as to whom I am perpetually astonished that I don't like him more than I do—rolled into one. Voltaire, too ! What expectations he arouses and what disappointment brings. *Candide* is very well for thirty or forty pages but overdone in eighty or ninety, and I have mined away for years at the *Philosophical Dictionary*, to be rewarded with surprisingly few nuggets. Swift is worth ten of him and Shaw twenty. But enough of these literary Struldbrugs.

For poetry I early decided that I had no affinity. If somebody would read it to me taking me, as it were, by the æsthetic hand and lead me gently and persuasively through its lusher pastures, along its more flowery paths, I could do with it well enough, but I had no independent drive towards it, and after the first fine flush of undergraduate rapture have rarely essayed to read it by myself.

The Admired Moderns

Secondly, there was the contemporary literature that was springing up all round me from the early 'twenties onwards. In the literature of the Edwardian age I had revelled, and prior to 1914 nobody could have been more contemporary in his taste. I read everything of Shaw, Wells, Bennett, Galsworthy, Chesterton, Belloc, and thought that there never had been such literature. I naturally expected that this enjoyment of contemporary work would continue after 1918, and can still remember the growing bewilderment with which I gradually accustomed myself to recognise that it did not. Huxley I liked though he shocked me, and E. M. Forster's *Passage to India* I thought a great book. But D. H. Lawrence never seemed to me to regain the pre-1914 form of *Sons and Lovers*, and it was only with difficulty that I taught myself to read and even enjoy the snapshot literature of Virginia Woolf.

When presently the literary roost was ruled by Joyce and Hemingway, each with his train of followers and imitators, I found myself for the first time out of touch with contemporary taste.

As the rather brittle gaiety of the 'twenties petered out in the gloom of the 'thirties, I found it increasingly difficult to obtain pleasure from contemporary literature. The sombre proletarian novels, the novels of atmosphere in which nothing ever happened, the novels in which tough "guys" expressed their savage emotions in ungrammatical sentences of squat monosyllables, the working class novels, the novels about half-wits, sexual perverts and children—these might have their interest for the politician, for the sociologist or the psychiatrist, but it was hard to think that anybody could read them for pleasure. Presently there was Kafka treading without gaiety or kindliness his long pilgrimages of fantasy and frustration ; later still, the novels and plays of the Existentialists in which again no laughter is heard and little story told.

At this point I venture with some diffidence to suggest four rules which guide my own taste in novels and short stories and which, as it seems to me, those who write them would do well to observe.

Rule 1. A novel or short story should have a beginning, and an end. There should, that is to say, be some perceptible reason why it begins, and there should be some other reason why, having once begun, it should end. In a word, it should have form.

Secondly, it should be *about* something. Its theme, that is to say, should be both definable and substantial. Love is such a theme, but it is only one among a number.

Thirdly, the English language is an adequate instrument for the purposes of intelligible expression. There is, therefore, no need to play pranks with its grammar and syntax, there is no need to invent new words, and there is no excuse for unintelligibility, which is usually the outcome of slovenly writing.

Fourthly, speculations by the author about the nature and purpose of the universe and the status of man within it, about the reasons for our presence on this planet, about the meaning of life and the right way to live it, have their place, but their place is not in a work of fiction. They should be reserved for works on philosophy, ethics and theology which have over the centuries developed certain techniques for dealing with and evaluating them.

Judged by these common-sensible rules much, perhaps most, advanced contemporary fiction fails. Joyce, for example, offends against the first and third ; Kafka against the fourth ; Sartre and Camus offend violently against the fourth ; so, incidentally, does Graham Greene. The great ruck of contemporary novels, particularly novels and short stories by admired English writers, offend against the first. They are novels of atmosphere and psychology ; they delve with infinite care into the consciousnesses of persons of no distinction and they convey with expert exactitude the atmosphere of places in which nothing of importance has happened. Most contemporary fiction at a slightly lower level is rendered unfit for the attention of a mature mind by its disregard of the second rule, for it is almost exclusively concerned with the great passion of love. "Will 'A' go to bed with 'B' or with 'C' ? " "Will she or won't she ? " "What does he feel for her and she for him ? " With the wearisomeness of an infinite monotony the changes are rung upon the comparatively limited variations of the dullest of the passions. For love, I insist, is exciting only to lovers. Than the love affairs of other persons what could be more unremarkable ?

1. *Not Reading What One Ought to Read.*

And so I come at last to the first of the pleasures of age. It is to have become so indifferent to contemporary taste that you no longer feel shame at reading what you like, instead of reading what you ought to like. *Lorna Doone,* now ; how I have loved that book ! I read it again every fourth year. *Guy Mannering, The Cloister and the Hearth,* the novels of Trollope, the major novels of Hardy—all these possess for me the supreme merit of telling a good story. (I don't mean, of course, that that is their only merit ; but it is the one held in lowest repute today and most conspicuously missing from contemporary literature.)

When young, recently adult or even middle-aged, I used to ration myself in respect of books that I really enjoyed, feeling that I must at all costs keep up with the times ; thus for many years I made my periodic and melancholy incursions into contemporary literature. But now I read unashamedly Dickens and Thackeray and the Brontes and George Eliot and Trollope and Jane Austen and Charles Reade and Wilkie Collins and early Wells.

Meredith I must admit I now find too much for me, but I still read, albeit with a diminishing fervour, the gods of my youth, Shaw and Wells and Galsworthy and Bennett. Of contemporaries, the only writer that I really enjoy, punctually consuming everything that he provides, is Somerset Maugham. What deftness and skill in construction ; what feeling for character and knowledge of human beings ; above all what a story-teller and—to cite the most neglected of all the literary virtues—how easy to read ! (Why, I wonder, should it be imputed as a merit to an author that he has *not* taken the pains to make the reader's job easy and agreeable ?) Formerly, when I read these writers, I did so with a guilty conscience—why was I *not* reading T. S. Eliot or Auden or, later, Sartre ?—so that there was a shade of defiance in my pleasure in them. Today I read them without let or hindrance, securely, even gloatingly, chuckling to myself the while because I am *not* reading the books that I ought to read.

The new books are published, the new books even come to the house, sent by their hopeful publishers but I, *I* am not reading the short story by Denton Welch, the novel by Graham Greene, the latest book on Existentialism by Sartre, or even Mr. Eliot's *Cocktail Party*. I am reading *Wuthering Heights* and I don't care who knows it ; or *Lorna Doone* or *It's Never too Late to Mend*, or *The Moonstone* or *Far From the Madding Crowd* or *Green Mansions* or *You Never Can Tell* or *War and Peace* or *Mr. Polly*, and so far from minding what anybody thinks about me, I am the rather given to making public avowal of my unregenerate tastes. In particular, I *don't* mind not being able to talk about the Sartre or the Eliot to the lady who sits next to me at the dinner table and is so relentlessly up to date. The longer I live, then, the m ore I enjoy the pleasures of *not* reading Rimbaud and Kierkegaard and Ouspensky and Proust and Rilke and Baudelaire and Buber and Berdyaev and Niebuhr and Faulkner and Mumford, not to mention my own countrymen for fear of offending them. It is a real pleasure that I derive from these abstentions, a private and personal pleasure, a pleasure of the self.

2. *Not Minding Being Left Out of the Party*

Which brings me to the second small compensation, such as it is, that I have found in age. I am not the sort of person to whom the world gives anything away. Some people can't abide me ; others distrust me and deem me unreliable. They are wrong in this, since nineteen twentieths of me, as I have said elsewhere, craves for respectability, position and respect. But that is not the part that eminent and respectable persons see ; moreover, one single outburst by the remaining twentieth bedevils the aspiring efforts of the other nineteen, sometimes for years, sometimes for ever.

I arouse violent partisanships ; while many regard me with dislike and contempt, some, not so many, are my warm adherents and untiring apologists. It is just as well, I have sometimes thought, that they are untiring. Not to put too fine a point on it, I am indubitably not the sort of safe man who wins people's confidence and is, therefore, continually being appointed and elected to positions of emolument and importance, who is promoted and given honours.

It follows that all my life I have been left out of things. I have *not* been put into the team, *not* made captain of the house, *not* been asked to join the headmasters' party on his yacht ; I have *not* been appointed secretary of the debating society, *not* elected to office at the Union, *not* made a member of this exclusive club or that snob society. In a word, then, I am habitually not elected, appointed or promoted and no person, body or institution is ever moved to suggest *me* for an honour.

And I have minded passionately. I am not tough and thick-skinned as people think, and perpetual slights by my fellow men have wounded me deeply. How I have minded being left out of the party !

And all the time I had to pretend that I didn't mind. Partly it was the pride that doesn't like the world to see how deeply it is hurt ; partly the training of my class which taught me to keep a stiff upper lip before the world, that led me to feign indifference, even to call sour grapes. The Labour Party would not nominate me for a constituency ; but I didn't care. "Who, after all, in his senses could wish to enter politics ? " I was passed over for the Presidency of the club which should have been mine by the right of order of seniority. "But who wants to be a figure-head," or, alternatively, "to be burdened with responsibilities and spend his time carrying out boring routine duties ? Much better to enjoy the privileges and amenities of the club without the obligations." For years I wanted desperately to be an Oxford don ; my applications were regularly neglected and younger men appointed in my place. But a don's life, I could plausibly maintain, passed in the comparative obscurity of a University town, was a life out of touch with the great world of affairs into which any man worth his salt must strive to enter, and so on. . . . There is no end to the devices of the rationalising intellect when it seeks to save the faces or salve the hurts of the emotions. Even to myself I pretended, persuading myself that I didn't mind when in fact I minded terribly.

There came a day some time in the middle fifties when some particularly pointed slight was administered. Here was something to which I manifestly ought to have been invited and I wasn't. *And I really didn't mind.* For some time I couldn't understand what had happened to me. Why no despondency, no angry resentment, no heart burning ? Was I putting up a show that deceived even myself? No, I concluded, the occasion was wholly new in kind. *I really didn't mind.* Here, then, at last was one of the compensations of age, a purely private and personal pleasure, the pleasure of not minding being left out of the party.

3. *Not Minding Emotional Dependence*

Of this third compensation I shall write briefly, for it opens a large theme, too long to be broached at the end of an already overlong chapter. All my adult life I have resented my dependence upon women. What slights, what humiliations, what ignominies, above all what boredoms have I endured because of my physical need of women. For, by and large, I have not liked women, greatly preferring the company of men. The generalisation, of course, is unfair. One subjects one's relations with women to a strain which no friendship with a man is expected to bear, the strain of continual intercourse *à deux*. In the beginning this is one's own fault. Nature or the Life Force or whatever it is that throws the sexes together from the age of twenty onwards, taking no heed of differences of taste, outlook, upbringing, class or temperament, but apparently concerned only with the fulfilment of her or its purpose, the continuance of the species through them—nature, I say, impels the recently licensed and possessing male to shut himself up alone with his new possession. The instinct is, I suppose, a survival in us of the habits of our palæolithic—or is it our neolithic ?—ancestors who, having won their women, carried them off to cave or hut. At any rate, so long as the hot fit lasts, one demands nothing more, one is satisfied with nothing less than this total companionship, this world-excluding enjoyment. In a word, one pairs.

But later the demand for an eternal *tête à tête* comes from the other side. The man, satisfied and by now a little bored, wants to resume the variety of his accustomed pursuits and to return to the company of his friends. He wants to play games, attend meetings, spend his money at club or pub in the company of his cronies. But women, whose instinctive attitude to the members of their sex is one not of welcome, but suspicion—every woman sometimes seems to see every other as a potential rival—do not, on the whole, desire to go out into the world, unless their man is with them. Nor have they facilities for entertaining themselves. Hence, the eternal cry of the neglected wife, "You never take *me* out with you ! " springing presumably from the implied premises that (*i*) she has no interest in going out with another woman, (*ii*) is not sufficiently attractive to win the notice of some other man and (*iii*) has not sufficient resources within herself to enable her to tolerate her own society.

Of all the many counts in my indictment of women, the painful regularity with which, once they have become attached to you, they make you responsible for their entertainment, so that to leave them for a few hours is counted a dereliction, a source of grievance and an excuse for eternal complaint, is by no means the least formidable. What boredom, what stifling and choking, what spiritual claustrophobia, as they insist upon your taking upon yourself the burden of the eternal company of their jejune personalities ! I have heard women blamed for fickleness, for their constant craving for change, for their ever renewed demands for some new thing. I have not found them so. My complaint would be rather of their highly developed talent for inflicting and sustaining the most devastating monotony.

The demand, first by the man and then by the woman,

for exclusive possession in comparative solitude imposes upon their relationship an intolerable strain. Upon the couple who live together, be they married or in sin, their descends a glass shade. To live under such a glass shade alone, or alone with a man, would be bad enough. But alone with a woman !

And so throughout my adult life I have looked forward to the time when I should be free of my dependence upon women. Well, that time has come, or nearly, as the claims of my physical nature begin to grow less exacting, soon to disappear altogether.

And am I pleased, am I grateful ? On the contrary. I look back wistfully to the days of my slavery and, as the physical chains wear thin, note the forging of a new set. For, behold, a surprising thing has happened. I am grown emotionally dependent. I begin to want women's society, to rely upon their companionship, to appeal for their sympathy. I take pleasure in their company. Sublimation ? Possibly. Dotage ? Perhaps. I think of that summary of marriage, one of Bacon's masterpieces of conciseness, a wife is a young man's mistress, a middle aged man's companion and an old man's nurse. Well, I suppose I am getting to the nursing stage, and what dependence could be more complete than that of the patient on his nurse ?

And if the nurse be kindly and compassionate and good-tempered, and if she love the petulant old reprobate—and women, thank goodness, have the faculty of lavishing their devotion upon the most unpromising specimens, the most unrepaying objects—then I rejoice that it should be so.

Here, then, is a third pleasure of old age—a pleasure private, personal, distinctive of the self ? I hope not. For I should hope that others may share my undeserved good luck.

CHAPTER IX

The Pleasures of The Pianola

Normality of Taste

I have pointed out on another page that even the oddest of us is in respect of nine tenths of himself normal ; which, of course, is why the remaining tenth of us is such an embarrassment to the rest. Most of the pleasures of the self described in this book have been an embarrassment. It is, therefore, with some considerable satisfaction that I come at last to a field of activity and enjoyment in respect of which I am a hundred per cent normal. In music my taste, albeit reactionary, is dead centre, a bull's-eye taste ! I like the great men, Bach and Handel and Haydn and Mozart and Beethoven and Schubert, and I don't like anybody else a hundredth part as much.

But though the music I admire is the same as that of other men—or, let me be candid, the same as that which men of taste admire—and though the pleasure I derive from it is, I imagine, very much like theirs, there is, nevertheless, one peculiarity which distinguishes my musical life, a peculiarity of approach. As this has affected my attitude to music as a whole, and as it has been responsible for a large proportion of the pleasure I have derived from it, this peculiarity may relevantly find a place in a work devoted to the distinctive pleasures of the self.

My approach to music is through the pianola. In this chapter I shall not, then, except incidentally, speak of my pleasure in Mozart or Bach or Beethoven, about whom I have nothing to say that has not been said a hundred times ; I shall confine myself to the distinctive pleasures conferred by the pianola.

Early Musical History

I am confirmed in this resolve by the reflection that I have no qualifications for writing about music proper. I can't play any instrument and I can't read a score. I can point to the note C on the piano and I can play from memory one or two pieces that Mr. Haddock[1] taught me, but this is the extent of my executive accomplishment. I am not interested in pianists and the technique of piano playing. I don't rush to occupy the front seats in the concert room so that I may see the movements of the pianist's hands. . . .

To set against these disabilities I have nothing to show save a passionate pleasure in and addiction to music, a pleasure so intense that when I was young it led me into all kinds of extravagances. Brought up to hear no music save the overtures patronised by Mr. Haddock[1], and the four Dances from *Henry VIII*, the selections from Gilbert and Sullivan and the *Peer Gynt* suite retailed in the Bournemouth Winter Gardens (Mr. Dan Godfrey) and on the piers at Brighton and Llandudno, when my sealed senses were at last burst open (incidentally, by an undergraduate at Balliol practising the last movement of Beethoven's Pathetique Sonata) I developed a voracious musical appetite which stuck at nothing for its satisfaction. I wanted, above all things, to hear great music played so that I might know what music there was, and I didn't mind very much who played it or how badly. My first wife could play a little—a study or two by a composer called Stephen Heller, some of the easier Chopin Nocturnes, Grieg's *Butterfly* and *Watchman*, and a piano arrangement of the inevitable *Peer Gynt* suite—and I bullied her into playing in and out of season.

In those days I was all for Beethoven—during the years 1916 to 1926, I used to go about saying that Beethoven had achieved in music a supremacy unequalled not only by any other composer, but by any other practitioner of any other art *in that art*—and I was agog to hear his sonatas. I can remember in particular my addiction to the last

1. See pages 24-26.

movement of Opus 31, No. 2 (Sonata 17), with its lovely, recurrent broken chord pattern, and to the second movement of Opus 2, No. 3, in which the left hand crosses the right to embroider a little figure in the treble.

But what nearly broke up an, at that time, happy marriage was that unfortunate Presto at the end of the first sonata, Opus 2, No. 1. The gracious minuet my wife could play fairly well, but the Presto was too much for her. Yet the Presto, which I had just heard at a concert, excited me beyond measure and I longed to re-hear it as the hind, or whatever the animal is, longs for cooling streams. As my wife's fingers stumbled haltingly over the notes, fumbled and broke down over those long running passages where the right hand trips all the way down from the treble to the bass, I used to dance about the room beside myself with impatience. "Hit the notes, woman, hit them ! Hit them hard ! " I cried. "Hit *any* notes." Nothing mattered but that I should hear the music somehow. In the end my poor wife would retire in tears. The first time I heard the Kreutzer Sonata (Adela Verne and Ysaye, of all unlikely combinations) and the fiery rhythms of that fierce first movement came tearing at my soul, I was so moved that I couldn't restrain myself. I fidgeted in my seat and beat time to the music. The tears rolled down my cheeks. Ultimately I made such a nuisance of myself to my neighbours that I had to go out into the corridor.

I mention these matters, not because they are noteworthy otherwise perhaps than as a young man's follies—and who shall say how much of my extravagant behaviour was not, at least in part, histrionic, a dodge to impose upon others and perhaps upon myself a recognition of the passionate intensity of my experiences?—but merely to show how important was the place which music came to occupy in my life. It was as if all my æsthetic sensibilities had been canalised along a single channel. I cannot remember a time when I did not include at least two composers in my list of the world's five greatest men—I was given to the compiling of such lists —although it must be confessed that they were not always the same two. I have already spoken of the extravagance of the claim that I made in the early 'twenties for Beethoven. It is humiliating to remind myself that from the middle 'twenties onwards I was making an exactly similar claim for Bach who, I asserted, had achieved a supremacy in music unparalleled by the practitioner of any other art.

Limitations of Taste

My taste in music has always been limited. If someone were to point out that the limits look very like prejudices, I should admit the fact and proceed to glory in the being prejudiced. For of what avail is it to be an amateur in art and what advantage has he over the professional, if he can't ever entertain and indulge his prejudices? It is only the expert and the critic who must make a show of being open-minded. (I should not, I hope, permit myself to parade my prejudices in my own subject.) Besides, it is an open question whether the whole corpus of what passes for musical criticism is at bottom any more than a rationalising of our prejudices and preferences, an elaborately disguised way of saying "I don't like this. I do like that." The smoker likes to persuade you that tobacco ash is good for the carpet, but we know that his argumentative blandishments mean no more than that he doesn't want to put himself to the trouble of finding and using an ash tray. Similarly, the contemporary critic will try to persuade you that the idioms of eighteenth century music are played out, when all that he means is that he is tired of hearing them. The ability to throw out a smoke screen of technicalities, the better to pass off his dogmatisms as judgments is one of the chief accomplishments of a critic.

For my part, having no pretensions to being either a critic or an expert, I can parade my prejudices. The music, then, that I wish to hear has a narrow chronological limitation. If all the music written after 1828 were abolished, I should not care a row of semi-quavers. It is also limited in space, being pretty well confined to a comparatively small area of Germany and Austria. The

century and a half of central European music which was
composed between 1685, when J. S. Bach, Handel and
Domenico Scarlatti were born, and 1827 and 1828 when
Beethoven and Schubert died, is my musical *floruit*.

The Pianola Introduced

I go back to my prancings behind my wife's back which
proceeded, I insist, from nothing more reprehensible than
a passionate desire to hear great music played, played any-
how as long as it *was* played. Hence, when about 1921, I
was first introduced by my friend Bernard Gilbert, at that
time Secretary of the Manor House Hospital, to the pianola,
I realised at once that it might do for me just what I wanted
done. In 1921 the pianola, though no longer in its heyday,
was still an instrument to be reckoned with. The 1914
catalogue of rolls available in the library established by the
Orchestrelle Company of the Aeolian Hall had run to some
620 pages. The rolls were listed and classified under
the names of the composers, and although there was a
regrettable Miscellaneous Section which included some
monstrosities known as Classical Mosaics—juicy bits of
Beethoven and Brahms which somebody had selected and
strung together on the same roll—the great bulk of the music
covered by the rolls was set out in a sufficiently musicianly
manner under its appropriate opus number, its K number,
or whatever the relevant mode of designation might be.
And the amount of music available was substantial. Here,
for example, were all the sonatas of Mozart and Beethoven
and the first twenty-four preludes and fugues from *The
Well-tempered Clavichord*. The list of Bach rolls occupied
four pages, of Chopin rolls thirteen, and so on. You paid
your subscription, ordered your rolls, twelve at a time, and
in due course they were set down at your door. You changed
them as often as you liked.

It was during the first world war that the gramophone
began to rank as a musical instrument. The rise of the
gramophone corresponded with the decline of the pianola.
The next catalogue, issued in 1922, was a visible and melan-

choly witness of the decline. It ran to 160 pages only, and the music, no longer arranged under its composers, was designated alphabetically under the *titles* of the "pieces" played, so that *Somewhere a Voice is Calling* (Accompaniment in F, Medium voice) immediately preceded *Sonata*, and the list of sonatas was succeeded in its turn by *Songs My Mother Taught Me* (Accompaniment in C, Low voice). There was an extensive gardening section featuring *In A Monastery Garden* (Characteristic Intermezzo) Ketelbey, *In A Chinese Temple Garden* (Oriental Fantasy), also Ketelbey, *In a Persian Garden, In My Neighbour's Garden, In the Garden of Memory* or *In My Garden* (*tout court*). The Mosaics now occupied two closely printed pages. More than seventy per cent of the so-called "classical" music listed in the 1914 catalogue had disappeared and been replaced by popular song hits or dance tunes. Titles, as I have said, were now the order of the day and the works of the great composers appeared wherever possible under names allegedly expressive of their contents. It was inevitable in the circumstances that Beethoven's Op. 27, No. 2, should appear as *The Moonlight*, Op. 13 as *The Pathetique* and Op. 28 as *The Pastoral*. The standard of musicianship observed in the presentation of music for the pianola had, it was obvious, declined with its volume, yet it was still possible as late as 1922 for a pianola recital or, more precisely, a pianola and piano recital of a four-movement Beethoven Sonata, Op. 106, to be given at the Aeolian Hall, two movements being played on the piano and two (by myself) on the pianola. The players sat behind a curtain and the audience, who had been told that a pianola was at work, were asked to say which movements were played by which instrument. A respectable number got the answer wrong.

By 1924 wireless was already well under way, and it was the radio that finally killed the pianola as a musical instrument. A number of rather desperate devices were designed to arrest the decline that they could not prevent. There were "Hand-played" rolls, that is to say, rolls cut, not to the music as the composer had scored it, but to the music as a particular pianist had played it. Rhapsodies were announced as played by Myra Hess, *Angels' Serenade* as played by Henry Bergman, and Chopin Ballades as played by Pachmann. But let the Company describe these things in its own words.

"Hand-played rolls" says its Catalogue, "differ from the ordinary roll in that whereas the latter is cut in strict time, the former are produced by a pianist whose actual playing, with all its slight variations from strict tempo, is transmitted to a cutting machine. Even in the hands of a not very expert player they are extremely pleasing to listen to, while those who study their instrument and give attention to arriving at artistic renditions [*sic*] will find them very interesting and enjoyable to play as they do not interfere in any way with perfect personal control." This, of course, was nonsense. If the roll renders the music as interpreted by pianist XY, it certainly cannot render it as interpreted by C.E.M.J., and the narrow but appreciable limits within which individual interpretation was possible—and it was precisely in the possibility of individual interpretation that, as I shall in a moment try to show, the attraction of the pianola for me consisted—were still further restricted.

From another development, known as the "duo-art" roll, the element of personal interpretation had disappeared altogether. You pressed a button and the electricity did the rest, causing the spool supporting the roll to rotate and the instrument to play the notes as the slits in the paper came over the holes punched in what is known as the tracker bar. The pianola, it was obvious, couldn't survive on these terms as a musical instrument. As mechanical as the gramophone and much more restricted in its range, the pianola rapidly subsided into a machine for the rendering of dance music. It is from this last phase that the common notion of the pianola as an utterly soulless instrument derives. And utterly soulless it was.

Today no company sponsors a library, issues catalogues or distributes rolls to its subscribers. Rolls can, however, still be bought from a company known as the Artona. The

Artona issues monthly bulletins of new rolls. The current issue for the month in which I am writing, March, 1950, is mainly devoted to popular song and dance hits. There are also Paul Jones's, Christmas carols and, inevitably, the Warsaw Concerto. There is a long list of waltzes, and I am glad to see that the *Merry Widow* and the *Blue Danube* are still going strong. "Classical music" [*sic*] is represented by *Liebestraum* and *Chanson Triste*. Good old Liszt ! Good old Tchaikowsky !

Development of the Pianola : *Some General Principles*

But the pianola could, it is obvious, have developed in the contrary direction. Instead of being rendered so foolproof that any fool could play it, it could have been enlarged in respect of range and refined in respect of delicacy of response. And this result, it was equally obvious, would be achieved not by putting more mechanism into it, but by taking out some of the mechanism that was already there, so that there would, for example, be a direct contact between the pressure of the foot of the player upon the pedal and the impact of the hammers upon the wires of the instrument. It was precisely in this direction that a few of us did, in fact, develop it. We limited the *mechanism* of control to the lever which varied the rate of rotation of the cylinder which supported the rolls and to the levers which, as in a piano, softened or sustained the sound of the hammers on the wires ; while for the rest, and in particular for the phrasing and such *nuances* of expression as we were able to contrive, we relied upon variations in the pressure of our feet upon the pedals.

The Mechanical Piano

I now propose to deliver myself of some remarks respecting the mechanism involved in playing and listening to a piano. This is formidable and complex. (*a*) The player sees a score and reacts to what he sees. (*b*) He wills to play it. (*c*) His will transmits—by what means we don't know—a message to his brain. (*d*) His brain transmits the message

157

through the nervous system to his finger tips. (*e*) The finger tips press upon pieces of ivory. (*f*) The impulses initiated by the declension of the pieces of ivory are transmitted mechanically through several jointed pieces of wood to hammers. (*g*) The hammers hit wires. (*h*) The wires vibrate. (*i*) Waves of sound travel through the atmosphere reaching in due course the place where our ear-drums are. (*j*) Passing through the outer-ear they impinge upon the ear-drum situated in the middle ear and transmit currents through the enormously complicated machinery of the middle ear to the inner ear. (*k*) The resultant disturbances in the inner ear (which take the form of ripples imparted to a fluid contained in the cochlea which, in their turn, impart a swaying motion to long hair-like threads, the cilia, ranged along the inside of the cochlea) are ultimately conveyed to the brain. When the brain has been suitably stimulated, we hear—again we don't know how—the sound of the note which has been played.

I have mentioned only a few of the enormously complicated processes involved in playing and hearing a piece played upon the piano, but I have said enough, I hope, to show how elaborate the machinery is. In the case of the pianola the machinery involved is the same with the exception that the impact of the hammers on the wires is caused to occur by currents of air which pass through holes in a bar of metal, the currents being initiated not by the pressure of fingers on keys but by the pressure of feet on pedals. In the piano case an act of will initiates the working of the machinery of brain, nervous system and fingers ; in the pianola, that of brain, nervous system and feet. I have deliberately phrased this account in such a way that the difference between the two sets of events is reduced to a minimum ; and so reduced it looks very small indeed. In practice, of course, it is very great, but it is, I venture to assert, a difference of degree and not of kind. There are a vastly greater subtlety and sensitivity, there is much wider scope for variety in the varying pressures exerted by ten finger and thumb tips, than there are in the pressures of the soles of two feet. But pianola playing affords *some* scope for all these things, for subtlety, for sensitivity and for variety in the way in which the soles press upon the pedals. Cut out as much as possible of the mechanism that separates the pedals from the hammers, play in slippers, as I do, practise assiduously and you will enjoy not, of course, the pleasure of the interpretative pianist, but a *soupçon* of a *nuance* of a ghost of an aroma of an adumbration of a tincture—I will put it no lower, lest I mix by implication even more metaphors—of the pleasure of the pianist.

The "*Mystery*" of Touch

I wish, secondly, to say something on the question of touch. It seems to me that a great deal of needless mystery which is at once the prop and the reflection of musical snobbery invests the subject of the pianist's touch. Concert addicts pride themselves on being able to recognise a pianist by his touch ; they profess, for example, to be able to distinguish the touch of Schnabel from that of Cortot and that of Cortot from that of Horowitz. They indulge in refinements and subtleties of perceptiveness, alleging, for example, that the style and touch of Schnabel, peculiarly appropriate to Beethoven, are unsuitable for Mozart and so on.

For my part, I would like to try the experiment of leading these experts blindfold into a concert hall in which one of these so easily recognised pianists was playing, and then to ask them which pianist it was. I wouldn't mind laying twenty to one that nineteen of them out of twenty, especially if they be gushing women, would be unable to tell me ; or that, if they did get it right, they would do so only by guesswork. So, too, with conductors. With what intimate *expertise* people discuss the respective merits and demerits of the different conductors. "My dear," they rhapsodise, "he was just too wonderful," "he" being, of course, not Beethoven but Furtwangler. "Yes, he is absolutely blissful. But, you know, I prefer Toscanini in the Sixth. His playing of the last movement ! ! " How they scream and gush about tempo, vitality, tone colour, harmonic values, sensitivity, vibrato, crescendo, sforzando and bombinando . . . as the stream of silly words comes pouring out of the silly lips. Drop me one of these rhapsodising snobs down through the roof of the Albert Hall with her back to the conductor—mercifully, though perhaps inadvisedly, breaking her fall—a conductor, moreover, who we will suppose to be conducting some musical "chestnut", the Jupiter let us say, or the Schubert C Major, and ask her who he is. How often, do you suppose, will you get a correct answer? For my part, having listened to music for nearly forty years, the most that I would assert is that I might on occasion correctly guess that the Mozart was being conducted by Beecham and the Beethoven concerto or sonata being played by Schnabel—and even so, I should be as often wrong as right.

Nothing in the foregoing should be taken to suggest (a) that there are not good performances and bad ones, (b) that the difference between them is not enormously important and (c) that I can *never* tell one from the other.

I suggest that there are three, and only three, factors to be taken into account as determinants of variations of touch. For what, after all, can a pianist do with a note? He can hit it with more or less strength ; he can leave his finger upon it for a greater or less period of time and he can withdraw it more or less sharply or lingeringly. There are three questions, then, and only three to be asked about touch : (a) How hard does the pianist's finger hit the note? (b) How long does he keep the note pressed down? (c) How fast or how slowly does he withdraw the finger? All the so-called mystery of touch can, I suggest, be reduced to the different answers to be given in the case of different pianists to these three questions.

When we transfer our consideration from the fingers touching the keys to the hammers hitting the wires as a result of their doing so, I am not sure that the facts which we have to take into account aren't simpler still, being reducible to two, namely, the greater or less degree of force with which the hammer hits the wire and the length of time during which it remains in contact with it.

In the case of the pianola player, the touch questions which can be relevantly asked appear to be two only—how hard does his foot press upon the pedal and for how long does it press ? The effects of his foot pressure are the same as the effects of the pressure of the pianist's fingers and thumbs, namely, the impact of hammers on wires and the variables which are involved, are the same, being the degree of force with which the hammer hits the wire and the length of time during which it remains in contact with it. There is, of course, a difference between the piano and the pianola in respect of the *origin* of the stimulus which causes the instruments to make their respective sounds. In the one case the origin is the pressure of the pianist's finger tips plus that of his feet ; in the other the pressure of the pianola player's feet. And the ten finger and thumb tips are, I have already admitted, capable of very much more subtle graduations of pressure than the feet of the pianola player. But the difference is, I repeat, one of degree and not of kind.

The object of this lecture is to demonstrate that though the pianola is a more mechanical and less subtle instrument than the piano, the difference between them is not adequately expressed by saying that the one is, while the other is not, a mechanical instrument. Moreover, there is an art in pianola playing. You can get better at it and by constant practice you can make your instrument a more sensitive medium for the expression of your intentions. To a very large extent, of course, you are bound by the conformation of the pattern of the slits in the roll and by the size and shape of the slits, but you are not *wholly* bound.

I hope that I have said enough to show that, though from the point of view of the listener, a good gramophone may be greatly superior to a pianola, from the point of view of the player the pianola has a certain advantage, the advantage, namely, of giving scope for self-expression which the gramophone lacks. Over the last thirty-five years, one of the most dependable and continuing pleasures of my self has been

L.   161

the pleasure of expressing the self in the rendering of music on the pianola.

Frederick Evans

I have spoken above of "we" and "us" and there were in fact three or four of us who "developed" the pianola, if I may repeat my rather grandiose phrase, on what we considered to be musical lines. We visited one another's houses and heard one another play. A disconcerting characteristic of the "developed" pianola was that the instrument turned out to be so individual, so personal and so apparently capricious that none of us could play another's instrument— not, at least, without a substantial spell of preliminary practice. This rather unexpected characteristic gave us pleasure since it placed a further and, it appeared to us, a final damper upon the exploitation of the pianola as a commercial instrument. Rolls were, of course, our difficulty. I have told how the rolls available in the libraries first of the Orchestrelle and later of the Aeolian Companies showed, as the years passed, a marked decline in quality. "Classical" rolls went out of commission and were replaced, in so far as they were replaced at all, by song-hits, selections, jazz and, later, swing.

By dint of careful selection and collection I ultimately accumulated a library of some three hundred respect-worthy rolls, but there was a great deal of music that I wanted to hear for which no rolls had been cut. It was about this time that Frederick Evans wrote to me. I had included a brief account of the pianola and its pleasures in one of my early books ; I had also dilated upon its defects, none of which have I yet got my heart high enough to mention. (One of the chief, by the way, was and is the difficulty of emphasising a particular note or notes as, for example, when one is trying to bring out the entry of one of the voices in a fugue, while soft pedalling the rest, the pianola tending to play all simultaneous notes equally loudly. The manufacturers had sought to overcome this difficulty by a device known as "the Themodist", whereby the note or notes which it was desired to emphasise were played a fraction of a second earlier than those with which they should properly have synchronised. As might be expected, this device was far from satisfactory and when clumsily executed, as it often was, ruined the music. There was also a method of soft-pedalling *accompanying* notes which depended on substituting a series of perforations for a single slit.)

Evans wrote that he had given some thought to the improvement of the pianola in general and of the Themodist in particular. He had one or two other things, he said, to show me, and invited me to come and have tea with him. "I am an old man" his letter concluded, "but I think I can still show you how the pianola ought to be played." I couldn't resist this and one afternoon made the journey from Hampstead to Acton by the North London Railway.

Evans was one of the most remarkable men I have ever met. He had been a famous bookseller in, I think, Ludgate Circus, where his shop was frequented by the leading literary men of his day, particularly by the pre-Raphaelites, most of whom he had included among his acquaintances. His house was still furnished in pre-Raphaelite style—curtains, wallpaper and carpet by William Morris and on the walls prints of pictures by Burne-Jones and Rossetti. Evans also possessed a book of plates of Rossetti's pictures and another book of his poems in the most gorgeous of pre-Raphaelite bindings, all inscribed "to my friend, Frederick Evans" in the handwriting of the artist. There was a Holman Hunt original, and there were books inscribed by Ford Madox Brown. There were letters from all the lot. The house was, in fact, a pre-Raphaelite museum.

Evans had lived through several strata of literary men and Shaw had been a frequent visitor to his shop. Evans had for Shaw an admiration verging on hero worship and seemed at one time to have been admitted to a degree of intimacy greater than that accorded by Shaw to most other mortals. Shaw treated him with his usual generosity and sent him copies of all his books as they came out. These, too, were inscribed "To my friend, Frederick Evans."

163

When Evans retired he had just enough money to make ends meet in decent comfort, but not enough to pay the debts of a relative who had failed in business in, I think, the United States. Wondering how to lay his hands on the necessary amount, Evans thought of his first edition Shaws and with some trepidation wrote to Shaw telling him of his difficulty and asking whether Shaw had any objection to his realising what he could on the books. Shaw replied "of course not, my dear chap, that is just what they are there for" or words to that effect, and Evans, who knew the first edition market inside out, sold the lot to the tune of some three thousand pounds.

When I came to know him, Evans was in the eighties, a small, square-cut, stocky man with a red face and bushy eyebrows, wearing a little tuft of beard on his chin. He reminded me of Samuel Butler, except that the blue reefer double-breasted jackets that he affected gave him a nautical air. He was extraordinarily vigorous and vital and talked nineteen to the dozen from the moment I arrived to the moment when he sat down to the pianola. When his talk excited him, which it frequently did, he would get out of his chair and bounce about the room like a garrulous balloon. He would come across some phrase in a leader in *The Times* or the *Daily Worker*—he took both papers—ask me what I thought of it and before I had time to open my mouth, would tell me what *he* thought of it, tell me with a great wealth of emphasis and detail.

When I first got to know him he was just coming to Spiritualism and had a way of bringing all topics, however remote, round to the question of our survival of bodily death, of which he was convinced. On this subject, indeed, he developed a kind of fanaticism and became rather a bore. For my part, I loved to hear him discourse on music, his tastes, though wider, being not dissimilar from mine. He taught me a great deal, taught me, for example, the worth of Schubert. He was also for some inscrutable reason an admirer of Rachmaninoff.

Evans and the Composers

Schubert was, for him, one of the four great composers, and one of the four great composers ever since he has been for me. At that time I had still to hear the great posthumous sonatas, the A Major, the B flat and the C Minor. Evans played them to me, discoursing the while on their points and virtues. "Listen to that melody," he would say. "No, not that one, stupid, the one that's just coming. Straight out of Heaven, isn't it ? " For Schumann, on the other hand, he had little respect : "How the fellow does pound away with that thick left hand of his ! " But Bach was his great love as, indeed, he has been mine ever since.

Evans would send a postcard, "Just played a new fugue of J.S.B.'s—a beauty. Come to tea next week and hear it." The discovery would be, let us say, the rarely played Toccata and Fugue for the Clavier in D Major—just as good, by the way, as the Toccata and Fugue in D Minor, that good old "chestnut" which has lost its bloom through overplaying. The D Major nobody knows, though I believe Rudolph Dolmetsch once used to play it on the harpsichord, where it sounded thin and stringy. (What an overrated instrument, by the way !) The piece as a whole is rendered memorable by some lovely bits of recitative which link together the two movements of the Toccata and also its second movement and the fugue. "Now keep still and listen," Evans would say as he played the thing; "He is going to say something. There you are. He's said it. As you see, it's a question. He is asking something of the universe, or perhaps it's of God. Are you all right underneath, all right really, he is asking ? Through all this bit of recitative he is waiting for an answer. He still, you see, doesn't know." And then the answer came, came in the form of a relaxation of a passage of prolonged tension—I don't know the technical musical name for this. "There now," Evans would say, " you can see it's going to be all right. Be comforted. You see now or, rather, John Sebastian sees, or I see—I think I'm getting a bit mixed up about *who* it is that sees and *who* is being comforted—that it *is* all right. But *what* comfort ! *What* tenderness of comfort ! "—and then came that lovely lilting fugue at the end, springing up so suddenly and sweetly out of the solemnities of Bach's assurance of comfort—"Just like a blackbird piping up in a bush in the garden."

Whenever he was moved by a piece of music—and it was rarely that he was not, for I never knew a man with a greater gusto of appreciation—Evans would punctuate his rendering of it with comments. One of the advantages of the pianola, by the way, is that you aren't so overwhelmed with the technical difficulties involved in hitting the right notes at the right intervals as to be unable to spare time and attention to notice what it is that you are playing and, if so minded, to descant upon its outstanding characteristics.

Evans called Bach his "bread and butter music", meaning that it was suitable for all times of the day and for every mood. So I, too, have found it. In general, it is of all music that of which you least quickly get tired ; even of the Air on the G String, of the Fugue at the end of the Fifth French Suite, of the first movement of the Italian Concerto, of the Toccata and Fugue in D Minor, or of "Jesu, Joy of Man's Desiring"—yes, even of these you don't get tired, though from the last perhaps you are every now and then glad of a little relief.

Evans's comments on performers, singers and conductors were as pregnant as his comments upon the composers ; as pregnant and far more caustic. As most of the subjects of his raillery are still alive, I omit them here. But I give one —on Sir Henry Wood—which I include, unjust as I consider it to be, in order to show Evans's style. We disagreed violently about Wood for whom I had and have a profound admiration, more particularly in that it was through him that many of us young people got our chance of hearing for the first time the world's great orchestral music. Evans, however, would have none of it. Mention of Sir Henry Wood's name would rouse him to a fury of disapproval and denunciation. "The man's a beast ! The man's a beast ! " he cried, jumping about the room in his excitement. "He gets young people to come and hear Beethoven's symphonies and then proceeds to murder them—the symphonies I mean. Those aren't Beethoven's symphonies and concertos that they hear ! They are distorted and mutilated so that their own mother wouldn't know them. And the young people, not knowing any better, go away thinking that this is what Beethoven is. With their tastes permanently warped. . . . For most of them, poor dears, never learn any better. The man's a corrupter of youth, sir ! He leads it up the musical garden path. He ought to be made to drink the hemlock."

The Photographer

One other characteristic of Evans remains to be mentioned, one that I should perhaps have introduced first, since it is for this, if for anything, that his name will be remembered— he was a first-rate photographer. I don't mean merely that he was a man who took good photographs. I mean that he was one of the pioneers[1] of photography who, I was told, had played a greater part in the development of photography as "an art-form" than any other man. It seems that there was some quality about these early "art" photographs that has subsequently been lost and has proved impossible to recapture. I have heard Evans's name mentioned by leading professional photographers with something like awe. They speak of "an early Evans" or "a late period Evans." Certainly those of his photographs which he showed me—and he had large albums full of them—seemed to me lovely. They were mostly of outdoor scenes, reeds by a river, Great Gable under a stormy sky or an old barn. One or two which I have in my possession do indeed possess some of the qualities of a picture, in that you can look at them every day as they hang on the wall and still notice them.

And so to the pianola which was the occasion of my meeting this remarkable man. His claim that he had introduced a number of improvements was justified. In the case of the ordinary pianola the feet perform a double

---

1 More precisely he was a champion of "pure" and "straight" photography.

function : (a) they provide the energy which causes the motor to work ; in other words they make the thing go ; and (b) they are responsible, as I have explained, for the phrasing, for the intervals between notes and for variations in the volume of sound. Evans had hit upon a device whereby the first of these two functions was performed by electricity—you switched on to the main by a plug—leaving the feet wholly free for the performance of the second. He had a nice little baby grand and he got some very good effects, though no better, I considered, than those which I produced myself. Moreover, his mechanism was always breaking down, whether through some inherent defect or because Evans was getting too old adequately to execute his own conceptions, I never discovered.

Tea with Evans

I would go over to Acton about four o'clock in the afternoon. Tea was administered to us by Mrs. Evans, a pleasant, placid woman who clearly regarded Evans as a genius who couldn't be judged by ordinary rules or held accountable for his actions like other men. During tea Evans talked. In the early years of our acquaintance his talk was mainly of music ; he spoke of the rolls he had cut, of the concerts he had listened to over the wireless and so on, but as the years passed his conversation came, as I have told, to concern itself increasingly with Spiritualism. I deplored this tendency and tried to laugh him out of it. As we grow older, I told him, our minds become matted with "God-webs" ; but this was not the sort of joke that amused him. After tea he settled down to play and I to listen to a programme of rolls which had been carefully planned in advance.

I wish I could convey the atmosphere of these occasions ; beginning with the journey by the North London Railway from Hampstead Heath Station to Acton Central, they seemed to lie outside the main stream of London life in the 'thirties which, for the space of an afternoon, was suspended. In spite of its electrification this railway seems like a survival from the Victorian age, so decayed are its stations, so forgotten the area which it serves—Canonbury and High-bury and Barnsbury and Kensal Rise. The atmosphere of survival was intensified by Evans's house. After a walk through one of those totally impersonal twentieth century suburbs, utterly undistinguished and indistinguishable from a score of others, one came to a row of square, solid-looking semi-detached houses of yellow brick, which stood like surviving rocks of Victorian solidity among the oncoming waves of twentieth century pink. At the back a factory had recently been erected and its smoke came blowing across the little garden where a lawn led down to a small statue which presided over a pool of depressed goldfish. One got the impression of something belonging to a vanished age that had strayed by mistake into the twentieth century, sorry that it had done so, but putting up a gallant rearguard action against this trivial, flimsy world that knew it not.

The Rolls

The furnishings of the drawing and dining rooms were, as I have said, largely pre-Raphaelite. The rest of the building was little more than a warehouse for pianola rolls. For the last thirty years of his life Evans had been cutting rolls steadily at the rate of about one every two days. He used to work a little machine rather like a printing press which punched holes in a roll of parchment paper direct from the score. The rolls spawned and sprawled all over the house to the scandal of Mrs. Evans. They were stacked on shelves in attics, they were ranged along the wainscotting of the floor and were piled in the lavatory and the bathroom. Great mounds of rolls half-blocked the passages. On Evans's computation there were between three and four thousand of them.

One day I proposed to him that he should cut rolls for the four or five of us who were interested in the pianola. He agreed, and for the last five years of his life he supplied us with a fairly continuous stream of rolls which we circulated among ourselves. When he died in 1943, nobody seemed to want his collection of rolls—one of the drawbacks to pianola rolls is the amount of room-space they occupy—and Mrs. Evans, who thought of moving to a smaller house, was anxious to be rid of them. I bought them for a song. I now possess nearly four thousand pianola rolls almost entirely devoted to the music of the great classical composers. There are, for example, all the clavier and organ works of Bach, all the piano sonatas and concertos of Beethoven, all the piano sonatas and concertos of Mozart. The collection includes all the piano sonatas of Haydn.

The rolls lie about in bags in attics and spare bedrooms waiting to be played, but there is far more music here than I shall ever play in my lifetime. This immense mass of music is like a great jungle by which I am surrounded in which, every now and then, I clear a little space, a place of sorted, played and labelled rolls. When I die, I suppose the rolls will be destroyed. It is a curious experience to pick out an unknown roll—a late Haydn piano sonata, let us say—wonder what it holds in store and proceed to play it in order to find out. One has the sensation of an explorer faring forth over an unknown musical sea.

And so at last I come to the advantages accruing to the pianola player, the enjoyment of which has constituted one of the most continuing and distinctive pleasures of my self.

Advantages of the Pianola : 1. Absence of Difficulty

First, for the pianola player there are no technical difficulties. He can tackle anything. He can play the last movement of the *Apassionata* without turning a musical hair ; he can play any fugue, however complicated ; he can play the Goldberg Variations, even No. 29, in regard to which I have heard Donald Tovey say that there were only two men alive who had the technique to play it properly, that one of them was himself and that he couldn't play it properly. For many years I was in the habit of playing one of the forty-eight preludes and fugues every morning before settling down to work. (I mentioned this once in an article or lecture and was astonished to read a few days later in some musical paper the following : "Professor Joad's worship of Bach is extreme, to say the least, for he tells us that every morning after breakfast he rarely fails to play through the whole of the forty-eight preludes and fugues on his pianola ! I am reminded by this of Compton Mackenzie's prodigious feat of hearing through without a break on several occasions the seven symphonies of Sibelius." I have a considerable appetite for Bach but there are limits.)

Bach is the music for the morning and the morning is for Bach, when one brings to him a palate unsullied by emotion and unscored by events. After many years' practice, I have perfected a morning routine. I normally wake at eight and ring for tea which comes with the *Manchester Guardian* and letters. (If I haven't rung by 8.45, it comes uncalled for). I read the paper and letters in bed, dress—no shaving, thank goodness—omit breakfast and go straight to the pianola, reaching it about 9.15 and play Bach. I have been through all the "Forty-eight" several times, taking them as they come. I can play the ones that pianists always play, like Nos. 8 and 22 in the first book and 31 and 45 in the second, and the ones like No. 34 in the second book that pianists always avoid. (What a fugue No. 34 is, by the way ; it is the one that has two endings ; it used to end with a major close, but the major close was later replaced by a minor half-close followed by a new ending of the most prodigious strength. I have never heard a pianist play it—I expect that it is fiendishly difficult—but I must have played it a score of times.) After half an hour on the pianola I go straight to my desk and write—write without difficulty or strain, write, in fact, like an angel or as nearly like an angel as I can contrive.

On Not Playing too Fast

The fact that I can play anything, and play it at any rate, renders me immune from the greatest temptation of the pianist, the temptation of showing off, and in particular of showing off his speed, as if there were some merit in sheer digital dexterity. I have a number of remarks in pickle for pianists, executants and performers, waiting to be taken out for their chastisement some pages later on. But let me point out here, following a hint given, I think, by Neville Cardus, that almost all performers and executants, whether pianists, orchestral players or singers, are extremely bad judges of a piece of music and that one of the reasons for this is that they are not impartial, their judgment being biassed by the difficulty or lack of it which they find in a particular piece. If they play it hardly, with strain and tension, they dislike it; if easily, finding in it many opportunities for showing off the brilliance of their technique, they like it and play it again and again. And most of them will insist on playing much too fast. I once heard an admonition delivered to a brilliant young pianist by that great violin player, Georges Enesco. He was delivering what purported to be a lecture on the interpretation of Bach ; but it was not so much a lecture as a continuing conversation. Enesco's talk, enriched by a life-time of musical experience, was delivered in broken sentences in several languages, and illustrated by constant recourse to the piano. As his mind rambled over the map of music, one thing reminded him of another, and as he called a thing to mind he played it. He seemed to be able to play almost anything from memory but one of his hands was, I think, crippled by rheumatism and he grew tired and wanted help. He had intended to play the second Partita throughout and, feeling it to be beyond him, called upon the young pianist to come to his assistance. She was one of the outstanding performers of the contemporary concert platform, admired, adulated, even worshipped—two young men that very morning had nearly come to blows about which of them should take her breakfast up to her in bed. She sat down and began to rattle away at a great pace. Almost at once Enesco stopped her. "Not so fast, not so fast young lady," he said. "Yes, we all know that you can do it. No need to assure us of that. That technique of yours ! But of course, we take it for granted. But this was not written in order to display you to the audience ; it is a conversation between Bach and his Maker and you should respect it as such. Just stop thinking for a moment of your piano playing and stop trying to impress us. We *are* impressed already—by Bach. So be a little kind and unselfish and give him a chance." I have never seen a young woman so taken aback.

Now I, who can play faster than any pianist, have no temptations in this direction, and I find that I habitually play Bach more slowly than most of the professionals. Also I am impartial in my judgments, having no technical axe to grind and not, therefore, being biassed either for or against a piece of music by any opportunities for personal triumph that it may offer, any technical difficulties that it may present or frustrations that it may have occasioned.

Musical Numerology

At this point I propose to break into my tale of the advantages of the pianola with an interlude on the subject of musical numerology, by which I mean the various methods which exist for referring to pieces of music and to defend the system in accordance with which, when referring above to one of the "Forty-eight" I used the expression "No. 34 in the second book" instead of "the Prelude and Fugue in E Minor", and referred to "the second Partita" instead of "the Partita in C minor", thereby declaring myself a musical ignoramus from the outset. For musicians know these pieces by their keys, and stare at me uncomprehendingly when I speak of "Number 34 in the second book". Yet numbers are, after all, the most convenient and suitable symbols for the purpose of referring to pieces of music, just as they are the most convenient and suitable symbols for the purpose of referring to anything else. They are clear and distinct ; there is no ambiguity about them comparable to the ambiguity of the reference to two different pieces of music which are written in the same key, and the layman understands them.

In order to throw into relief the advantages of numbers, I bid the reader reflect for a moment upon the welter of confusion in which musical numerology lies wallowing, the welter which was first forced upon my attention by the

Pianola Companies' catalogues. Take Mozart's sonatas, for example. They are listed in one catalogue as numbered in Peters's Edition ; in another, according to Pauer's numbering in Augener's Edition. A third gives the Kochel number ; a fourth refers simply to Mozart's sonata in A as if there weren't two or three sonatas in A—as to which I don't know whether there are or not, but I do know that there are five piano concertos in B Flat and three at least in C Major, and how disconcerting it is, when you are expecting to hear one of them, to be surprised by the strains of a totally different one. The consequence is, of course, that you can never be sure what sonata it is that you are selecting to play. The Beethoven situation is a little better owing to the arrangement of his music under opus numbers, but even here confusion arises from the fact that several works may be listed under the same opus number, the six quartets of op. 18, for example, or the two 'cello and piano sonatas of op. 102, and when we come to the ragbag of the posthumous works with their simple denomination of Op. Post., there is at present practically no mode of identification except by reference to the key.

The Bach position is quite hopeless. As there are no Bach numbers, there is no standard of reference and I have known a piece of Bach referred to in the pianola catalogues in four different ways. And what are we to make of the all too common catalogue designation, "Organ Chorale Prelude" (without key or number) "Part II arranged by Busoni" ? And if you say, what else can you expect from those engaged in cataloguing music for so unscholarly and so unmusical an instrument as the pianola, I would ask you, what are *you* going to do by way of referring to the two Toccatas and Fugues in D Minor, the famous one and the other which is just as good as the famous one, and if you can't answer, let me tell you that in the absence of numbers you would be equally gravelled by the necessity of designating any one of a score of Bach's clavier and organ works[1].

1. I am told (November, 1950) that a standardised list and numbering of Bach's works has recently been compiled and published in Leipzig and that the first copies are just trickling through to this country.

What is wanted are a general cleaning up and standardisation of musical numerology. The obvious method is to list all the works of a composer in chronological order and give to each work its appropriate opus number with a list of additional separate numbers in the case of works falling within the same category ; in other words, to apply to music as a whole the same system as that which is used for Beethoven's music, care being taken to eliminate the confusion arising from sub-opus numbers. One could then refer to an Organ Prelude and Fugue of Bach's as Op.—, Prelude and Fugue (Organ)—while Preludes and Fugues for the clavier would be listed as Op.—, Prelude and Fugue (Clavier) — and so on. The job should be undertaken by an international committee, preferably sponsored by U.N.E.S.C.O., on the model of that set up by the League of Nations Committee for Intellectual Co-operation before the war for the establishment of a standard numbering and grading of the different colours. Short of an international committee, the job should be delegated to one of those painstaking committees of beaver-like American scholars.

Advantages of the Pianola ; 2. Formation of Taste

To return to the advantages conferred by the pianola, I propose to include the formation of musical taste. Let us assume, first, that some music really *is* better than other music[1]; secondly, that few of us can comprehend and appreciate first rate music the first time we hear it. (In case this sounds dogmatic, let me defend myself once again with the authority of Sir Joshua Reynolds : "Taste does not come by chance or nature ; it is a long and laborious business to acquire it. It is the lowest style only of arts, whether of painting, poetry or music, that may be said in the vulgar sense to be naturally pleasing.")

Let us assume, thirdly, and in consequence that you require to hear a piece of music a considerable number of times before you can tell whether you *really* like it or not

---

1. As this is not a work on philosophy, I don't propose to defend these assumptions. An elaborate defence will be found in my book *Decadence*.

since, if you like it the first time you hear it, the betting is that it will be second-rate. Now the advantage of the pianola is that it enables you to do a piece of music justice through hearing it many times, hearing it, in fact, sufficiently often to enable you to establish to your own satisfaction whether you really do like it or only thought that you did.

The changes in his taste that the pianola player records are many and curious. They mortify pride and give food for thought. I have already referred to the habit of the composers of pianola rolls of stringing together on a roll a number of juicy bits by the same composer and calling them "Classical Mosaics." Less reprehensible is a tendency to select three or four movements from a suite, say a Prelude, a Courante and a Gigue, and include them on one roll, omitting the intermediate movements which are deemed to have no immediate appeal. Or a roll may contain a Toccata from one Suite and conclude with a Gigue introduced as a fill-up from another. Common to all these cases is the inclusion on the same roll of several more or less unrelated pieces of music. Of these the first may on first hearing appear to you to have a moderate degree of attraction, while the second strikes you as dull and boring as only Bach *can* seem dull and boring ; the third, we will suppose, ravishes you. Let the third, then, be a Gigue, the Gigue, for example, with which the first Partita concludes. I defy anybody to hear this and not be ravished and ravished at once. Now the limitations of the pianola roll are such that the player cannot have access to the third without playing through the first and second.

It is significant to observe how with repeated playings the relative positions in one's favour of the three movements would gradually change. Instead of hurrying through movement No. 2, which we will suppose to be an Adagio, in order to reach No. 3 as quickly as possible, one would find oneself becoming interested in No. 2. Presently, one began to linger over it. A time came when one would find oneself actually looking forward to it, while No. 3, for the sake of which the roll was originally played, began to seem superficial—or rather, for I am writing of Bach and superficial is a word hardly applicable to any work composed by him — began to wear a little thin, assuming that rubbed and faded aspect of music which has been grossly overheard. (And in the case of other composers how trivial, how vulgar, how even meretricious have often seeemed one's early loves). In the end one didn't even bother to finish the roll. Thus, whereas one had begun with a ranking of Nos. 3, 1 and 2 in order of favouritism, one ended up with the ranking, 2, 1, 3.

As examples, I cite my changes of attitude to Bach's Toccata in G Major—at least that is what Evans called it, but it may be, for all I know, a series of pieces strung together by himself—in which the lovely adagio which constitutes the third movement came gradually to oust in favour the sparkling merriment of the Allegro with which the Toccata begins, and the Toccata and Fugue in D Minor (the other one) in which the originally despised Adagio again caught up with and finally outstripped the rest of the roll.

The pleasure of learning to like new music in this way is very great ; but the pleasure is not all ; one is taught— if it isn't conceited to say so—humility. One learns (a) how unworthy are one's initial and untutored likes and dislikes, how almost infallibly one begins by liking the wrong thing, and (b) how very wrong one can be at all times. It is, I suggest, a sound principle of musical listening, a principle which holds good at any rate for most of us, that no first-rate music should ever be heard for the first time, for the first time it will bore and bewilder you.

I have already quoted Sir Joshua Reynolds to the effect that it is only the lowest style of the arts "that may be said in the vulgar sense to be naturally pleasing." Let me reinforce with Walter Pater's "The way to perfect taste lies through a series of disgusts." These truths are not understood in the age of the common man who has been brought up to think that there is nothing that he can't understand, nothing that he can't appreciate at first hearing —are not his understanding and his taste as good as anybody else's ?—and that he has only to approach the best that has been thought, read, said, written, painted and composed for it to fall into his mouth like a ripe plum. "The ripe plum" fallacy is reinforced by the weakness of one's own musical flesh which will not permit one willingly and wittingly to inflict Walter Pater's "disgusts" upon oneself. Hence my gratitude to the pianola which imposes them upon me, as it were, by force, compelling me to listen to and ultimately to be conquered by the initially unpopular but intrinsically superior work which insists upon being played through before one comes to the initially popular but intrinsically inferior work for the sake of which the roll was originally chosen.

Advantages of the Pianola ; 3. The Range of Music

On Musical Chestnuts. It was only after Evans had been cutting rolls for me for some years that I realised how extremely restricted in range is the music that is played upon the concert platform. Again and again the same old pieces recur. Taking into account only the orchestral or concerted works of the "great four", we hear again and again the Beethoven symphonies, the G Minor and the Jupiter, the Brandenburgs, the Bach Double Violin Concerto, the Italian Concerto, the Schubert Unfinished and (less frequently) the Schubert C Major, Mozart's Violin Concerto in E flat Major, and most everlastingly recurrent of all—the Beethoven Violin Concerto in D and the Emperor.

As for the pianists, they serve and re-serve interminably the more brilliant Preludes, Etudes and Nocturnes of Chopin, the Beethoven sonatas, particularly the earlier ones, but scrupulously avoiding Op. 101, most, but not all, of the first volume of The Well-tempered Clavichord and precious little of the second. When one thinks of the enormous corpus of music that is in fact available for playing, neither better nor worse, neither harder nor easier of approach and appreciation than this time-honoured array of well-worn chestnuts, one is astonished at the arbitrariness of the pianist's selection.

Why is not more heard ? Why, for example, Bach's

Fantasia and Fugue in A Minor but not the Fantasia (no Fugue) in A Minor. Why the Prelude and Fugue for the Organ in A Minor but not the Prelude and Fugue for the Organ in A Major ? Why do we hear over and over again the Organ Prelude and Fugue in G Minor but never the Fantasia and Fugue for Organ in A Minor[1]—a terrific ending to the fugue of this last which is as impressive (in fact the whole fugue is just as impressive) as the everlastingly played Prelude and Fugue in A Minor, as to which, in the old Hand-played Rolls days[2], I possessed "renditions" by no less than three famous pianists. Why are the Air and Variations in A Minor so persistently neglected ? Think for a moment of music as an ocean ! Then the contemporary platform performer lets down his thimble—nay, let me be just, his bucket—brings it up and pours its contents upon his audience, pours not once but over and over again. Or think of a Stilton cheese. What is played is a little cave in the cheese which has been hollowed out by a spoon and served up for our sampling. Nor would we complain, for after all one's aptitude for sea water and Stilton cheese is limited, were it not always the same bucketful, the same spoonful—or pretty nearly.

When one does complain to performers, they lay the blame on the public. The only way to attract a good audience to a concert of good music, as opposed, of course, to a concert by a star performer, is, they say, to serve up musical "chestnuts", the Emperor, the Fifth, a Little Night Music, and so on. Depart from the accepted repertoire which the public knows and you will play to half empty seats.

I have known in my time many societies which were formed for the express purpose of performing the lesser known works of the great composers, but none of them lasted long. Mr. Jay—or was it Mr. Pomeroy ?—lasted longest, giving Sunday evening concerts of "non-chestnut" Mozart and Schubert—the Schubert Piano Trio Op. 100, for example, and not the Piano Trio Op. 99—which lasted through the

---

1. This is not any of the A Minors just referred to but a different one and constitutes a good example of the appositeness of my remarks on musical numerology. 2. See p. 156

whole of one winter. But Mr. Pomeroy—or was it Mr. Jay ? —was a rich man and he was much poorer by the end of the season.

All this is true, yet, even so, I wonder whether the performers couldn't sometimes be a little more adventurous than they are. It is hard enough, God knows, for Miss XY, straight from the College or the Academy, to make her way upon the concert platform ; inevitable, in the circumstances that she should play for safety. But why, when she does voyage out upon an uncharted sea, should she inflict on us some contemporary monstrosity, some chromatic horror by Hindemith or Stravinsky, or an outpouring by one of those frenzied Russians, Shostakovitch or Kachaturian ? Why not some uncharted Bach ?

In my time I have played uncharted Bach to three young women professionals, begging them to introduce at least one novelty to their audiences. One refused ; one, to whom I had played the Bach Clavier sonata in D Minor—the one with the lovely last movement in which for once Bach unbuttons himself and lies sprawling after a metaphorical drink or two under a hot sun on the river bank—played it and was complimented by the critics. The third, to whom I played two problem pieces—one by Bach, rather broody and entitled (presumably by Evans) Fragment for Clavier, and the other, that extraordinary Fantasia and Fugue of Mozart's in C Major (K.394)—(I don't mean the Fantasia and Fugue in C Minor (K.475) which quite a number of people know)—which begins by sounding like Mendelssohn and goes on through Cesar Franck to Beethoven, while the fugue is apparently pure Bach—I have again to thank Evans for this musical curiosity—tried them out on an audience, announcing them on the programme according to my recommendation with a note of interrogation instead of the composer's name, and circulating slips among the audience asking them to insert the names if they could. She came, I am sorry to say, a most awful "flop". The critics denounced the whole proceeding, perhaps because there were no prizes for the correct answers, while the public, a certain small number of whom had turned up at this pianist's previous concerts, dwindled after this one practically to nothing. I suppose people didn't like being shown up.

A Successful Novelty. But I have had my successes as well as my failures. My first writing about the pianola hooked not only Evans but that admirable Bach player James Ching. In this writing I denounced most Bach players because of their flagrant disregard of my "clean pane" theory—I shall come to this in a moment, but briefly what it means is that the pianist should seek to turn himself into a transparent window pane, transparency involving in this connection the maximum suppression of personality. Ching wrote to tell me that I didn't know what I was talking about. "If you want to hear Bach as he ought to be played," he said in effect, "come and hear me." I went, and he was abundantly justified. Excepting only Claud Biggs and, at one time, Harold Samuel, Ching was the only pianist I had heard who played Bach just as I considered he ought to be played ; that is to say, Ching's Bach came out crisp, bright and dry when it ought to be crisp, bright and dry, and grew meditative and contemplative when Bach is contemplating the universe, meditating upon what he finds and recording his meditations. The thing was all Bach and no Ching and since, if music could write itself, it would, I imagine, sound pretty much like Bach, I might almost say that it was all music and neither Bach nor Ching.

I came to know Ching well and listening to his playing became one of my greatest musical pleasures. He was a good cook and would ask me to lunch, when we would have an omelette and a bottle of Moselle prior to a Partita. One day, exploring in the Evans jungle, I came across the Prelude, Fugue and Allegro in E flat. I was enthralled by it, the prelude so divinely calm, with a tranquillity matched only by the Prelude of No. 38, Volume II, of the Well-tempered Clavichord, the fugue so decisive and bold and the variations on the fugue's theme so exciting. I disapproved at first of the Allegro, thinking it bright and rather empty, but later became reconciled, though it never occupied in my heart more than its third place on the roll. I played the thing to Ching—as a matter of fact he says that it was *his* discovery and that he played it first ; but I don't believe a word of it. He was as pleased with it as I was and played it with great success on the concert platform and also in a broadcast programme. Later Ching started a piano school and caused his pupils to practise it. The school was a success, the pupils prospered and presently the Prelude, Fugue and Allegro were outcropping all over the concert platforms of London.

But I have wandered from the "advantage" of range. Let me, then, say that there is no door anywhere in the piano, chamber and concerted music of Bach, Handel, Haydn, Mozart, Beethoven and Schubert that is closed to me. Even Haydn's Sonatas, most of which nobody knows and which are uncountably many—even Haydn's Sonatas are accessible to me. I have played all the piano and violin sonatas of Mozart in arrangements for the piano and, though lacking the violin these are but halt and maimed, yet they are in themselves so lovely that they repay even a pianola rendering. (They are much better than the Mozart piano sonatas, and Mozart himself cared more about them. Why, then, don't the silly performers play them, and why don't they play the piano and violin sonatas of Handel?—first rate stuff as Handel always is, though not in the same class as the Mozart.)

Advantages of the Pianola : 4. That You Can Hear What You Want to Hear Both Before and After.

(*a*) *Before.* As I have already pointed out, no good music should be heard for the first time. But if you have a pianola it needn't be for the first time. For you can overhear it unofficially, before you hear it officially. One of Evans's few lapses of taste, as I considered, was his willingness to tolerate chamber music, trios, quartets, quintets and so on and even symphonies on the pianola, whereas I hold the pianola to be in general intolerable save for piano music. When I taxed Evans with this, he defended himself by saying that he had found it helpful before hearing a new work or one with which he was imperfectly acquainted, to play it through before going to the concert at which it was to be performed. One visualises its outline, he said, and sees its proportions ; sees it, as it were, in perspective. As a non-score reader I, too, have found this a great advantage.

(b) *After.* I will confine myself to one example of "hearing after". At the musical summer school at Bryanston in the summer of 1948, I heard William Glock lecture on Mozart's piano concertos. I knew the concertos pretty well, but had never heard them expounded. Glock is the almost perfect lecturer on Mozart. He is a professional musician who knows what he is talking about ; yet he succeeds in remaining non-technical, and he is sufficiently master of his subject to be at play with it. Also he loves the music on which he lectures and can communicate his love to his audience. He seems to be able to play almost anything from memory and his illustrations on the piano, showing the entry of the various themes and subjects, their development and the modulations from key to key, are a constant delight. One lecture was illustrated throughout by particular reference to the C Major Concerto. I don't know how many C Majors there are. I was fairly well acquainted with two, but this one was new to me, being, in fact, K.504. When he came to the last movement he mentioned, as it were in passing, a particular subject, the second—or was it the third ?—one of those heavenly little bits that Mozart scatters so generously all over his work, a something over, an ἐπιγιγνόμενον τί, given to you out of his abundance. "This" said Glock "is one of my favourite tunes in Mozart." He played it. "Well, there you are," he commented, "It's lovely, isn't it ? " And so it was, lovely. I hoped to hear it again, but Mozart had, it appeared, mentioned it only in passing and passed quickly on to discourse of something else. I couldn't rest musically until I had heard it again. When I got home, I began to search in the Evans jungle, found the Concerto, took it out and played it, played it, indeed, again and again so that I did violence to it and cursed myself afterwards for my intemperate, musical habits.

Advantages of the Pianola : 5. *That You are Active, That You Can Turn Back and That You Can Repeat*

When you are ill or convalescing from illness there comes a time when you tire of both wireless and gramophone. Listening to good music is, God knows, a good thing, but it is a passive thing. The effect of most great music on me is to engender a wish actively to participate, and if I can't actually participate in the music at least to "go and do something" about it, remove mountains, lead lost causes, enter a monastery, become Prime Minister or walk twenty-five miles. There are times when I would sooner take a part in singing songs at the piano, sooner join in a round, than listen to the greatest music that was ever written played by the most celebrated performer that ever there was, which is, perhaps, why Mr. Britten's famous device of dividing up his audience into sections in order that they might the better participate in the singing of the choruses of his *Let's Make an Opera,* contributed so greatly to the justifiable popularity of this pleasing work. One wants, then, to be active and take part and, save for turning the knob, save for choosing the record and putting it on, the wireless or gramophone listener takes no part. Now the pianola is an instrument that you play yourself and, as I have already tried to explain, you can put something of yourself into the playing ; you express yourself, therefore, and you are active.

Again and again I have come back from a concert, gone straight to the pianola and had more pleasure from the playing of the instrument, putting my foot down hard to bring out this note, gently caressing the pedal for that one, bringing out the theme with the most delicate pressures and agitations of the sole, than ever I had from the concert. Again, one's pleasure in music is apt to be capricious and uneven. Admired pieces bore you—many of the slow movements, the sentimental ones, of Mozart's piano sonatas

184

and concertos bore me ; so does the Hammerclavier, so does the last movement of the Ninth Symphony and the slow movement of the Eroica. Others delight you past all measure and reason—for example, in my own case the slow movements of Nos. 2 and 3 of Mozart's violin and piano sonatas, the Larghetto of Beethoven's Seventh Symphony, the whole of Beethoven's Op. 96 piano and violin sonata so pastoral, so meditative, so sheerly beautiful, or the last movement of Schubert's posthumous B flat sonata.

In a word, one has one's individual preferences and dislikes in music as in anything else. Some music is one's particular "cup of tea", other music most emphatically is not. Even within the same movement some things are better than others. The great composers strike one at times as being singularly un-self-critical. They will toss off something so inexpressibly lovely that physical *frissons* of pleasure run up and down your spine. Expectantly you look forward to the return of this loveliness but, alas, it doesn't return ; what does return is the everyday, bread and buttery main theme of the movement. The great composers, in short, often don't seem to know when they are "on to a good thing" or how infinitely better are some of the things that they dash off and dwell on for a moment only, than others in which they apparently take a vast pride. Examples could be given by the dozen. I have already referred to one of those fleeting, unrepeated little tunes that has embedded itself almost by accident halfway through the last movement of Mozart's C Major Concerto, K.504. There is the no less lovely theme, so fresh is it, so lyrical, so spring-like, that occurs in the first movement of the C Major concerto, K.467, though this is admittedly vouchsafed to us twice.

Or consider the bunch of lovely little tunes that come jumping out at you in the last movement of Mozart's Piano Quartet in D, so many, so sunny and so dancy that you might swear a fountain was at work spraying them all over the room, one, so much sunnier and dancier than the rest that you would give your ears to hear it again. But you don't. I scarcely ever hear a Minuet of Mozart's without thinking how much better is the Trio than the main Minuet theme—so, too, in those edgy Scherzos of Schubert, there are some heavenly Trios—but the main Minuet theme is repeated sometimes, as it seems, to eternity and takes up, at the least, three or four times as much time as the Trio. But the most outstanding and familiar example of this lack of self-criticism occurs in the last movement of the Beethoven Violin Concerto. The main subject, so rude and coarse— Falstaff guffawing as he straddles in his armchair with his pint beside him, his fly-buttons undone and a belch or two among the guffaws—comes again and again[1]. This is Beethoven in his unbuttoned mood, poking you in the ribs until you long to tell him to have done. And then quite suddenly without any warning comes the exquisitely lovely second subject. Appearing as it does in the midst of the jollity, its eloquent beauty thrills while it saddens you, saddens you but with how delicious a woefulness. The theme, comparatively short, is repeated ; you hold your breath, it is so lovely, and then before you have time to recover it, Beethoven is back again at the guffawing and the belching. Beethoven, more than any other of the great composers, save perhaps Schubert, seems to me to lack self-criticism.

Now the purpose of these examples is partly to enable me to enjoy the pleasure which recalling these lovely things brings but, more relevantly, to include among the advantages of the pianola the ability to turn back and to play back. You can't stop the wireless ; to stop the gramophone and find the right place on the record makes a horrid noise and is bad for the record ; but nothing is easier than to stop the pianola, re-roll, find the place at which you began to be thrilled—you can even mark it in pencil—and play again. You can recognise the place on the pianola roll by the visual pattern of the holes and slits. And here accrues another advantage. With many of us—

[1]. Have I just entered a *caveat* against the use of literary similes and metaphors and do I stultify myself? Well, then, I stultify myself.

I am one—the eye is quicker at picking out a pattern than
the ear. You recognise a visual pattern of holes and slits
when you wouldn't recognise a subtle and much embedded
theme. By following the visual pattern and turning back to
it, I have taught myself, I will not say to understand, but
to find my way about in difficult pieces of music which
otherwise had baffled me. Were it not for the pattern of
the slits, I should never, for example, have learned that there
were three separate subjects in the fourth fugue of the Well-
tempered Clavichord, Book I, or learned to pick them out.
In all these ways playing the pianola is analogous to reading ;
and its advantage over wireless and gramophone is the
advantage of reading a play to yourself as compared with
the best performance of the same play in the theatre or over
the air.

Advantages of the Pianola : 6. *That It Provides You with a Ready
Made Test of Music*

Defects of the Pianola. The ability to turn back, coupled
with the ability to play anything that you want to play and,
such being the weakness of one's musical flesh, the failure
to resist the temptation to over-play it, put music to a
severe test. And—let me be frank about it—the pianola
itself puts music to a severe test. For when all is said that
can be said in its favour, the pianola remains a sadly un-
responsive instrument. It can give no satisfactory account
of any music except piano music and, except in the hands
of an expert, its rendering even of that is intolerable. It is
in any event tolerable only when you can bring a fresh mind
to it, which means that it is best played in the morning. It
is also most suited to what I have called "morning music",
the music of Bach, Handel and Scarlatti.

Nor are these the only limitations. I have hitherto
praised the pianola, as though it were an almost flawless
thing. Let me now confess some of its defects. All the
devices that I have mentioned[1] to bring out important notes
while softening others which are being played simultaneously

---

1. See page 162.

are more or less inadequate. A skilled performer like my-self can, by varying the pressure of his foot, do something to emphasise a particular note or a particular theme, but not very much. There are constant "tracking" difficulties, caused by the failure of the slits in the roll exactly to corres-pond with the holes in the metal tracker bar through which the air passes. There are various devices for overcoming these, but, once again, none is completely satisfactory. The margin of error in the case of the eighty-eight note rolls is so tiny that the least maladjustment, the fraction of a fraction of an inch, results in the note not being played or being only half-played. Indeed, the hair-breadth accuracy with which the slits in the roll are required to adjust themselves to the holes in the bar reminds one of nothing so much as the refinements of the dentist in adjusting what he calls one's "artificial dentures". As you never know when the roll may not be going to "get out of the true", you play in a state of constant apprehension—at any moment, you feel, the thing may "go off"—and the mood of apprehensive expect-ancy militates against the establishment of the state of mind, clear, tranquil and unsullied by emotion which is necessary to the full appreciation of the music. In the sixty-five note rolls the margin of error is wider, but so, too, are the slots in the rolls. In the case of long, sustained chords they are too wide, the roll is apt to crumple and not only are the intended notes played but the two immediately neighbouring notes, with effects of such novel discordance that they are justly envied by many contemporary composers.

But more important than these technical difficulties is the relative failure of the pianola to render with even approxi-mate adequacy certain *kinds* of music. I have spoken above of the happy impartiality of the pianola player. I have represented him as being not biassed by the frustration of difficult pieces or tempted by the brilliance of "showing off" pieces. But as usual I have exaggerated. He *is* biassed against the kind of music that the pianola renders with a more than average inadequacy. This is the kind of music which relies predominantly for its effect upon harmonic colour and tone values. Brahms's overladen and highly chromatic chords sound horrible on the pianola which is, no doubt, one of the reasons why I dislike him : so, too, does the noisier Chopin, the Scherzos, for example, and the bravura passages of the Ballades.

Structure in Music. In general, the pianola is hard upon music that lacks structure. It tends to throw up into high relief what might be called the bare bones of the music and, just as in the case of the human figure, it is the underlying structure, the shape and proportions of the bones in their relations, that confers grace, and just as, where grace is lacking, no amount of surface beauties, of texture of skin, of colouring or complexion can make up for its lack, so in the case of music structure, I have come to think, is the root of the matter. It is not so much how music sounds, the pianola has taught me—for on the pianola no music sounds very well —but how it is arranged that counts, so that its affinities are less with literature and the arts that have meaning and express emotion, than with chess and mathematics which, like it, depend upon order and arrangement. Now, it is precisely on the counts of order and arrangement that the pianola scores, since it plays the right notes in the right order and at the right intervals ; and of how many pianists can that be said ? And that is why contrapuntal music in general and the music of Bach and Handel in particular are pre-eminently suitable for the pianola. Which is, no doubt, partly why I like them so much.

When you come to think of it, it is first rather than second rate music that can stand up to playing which is below the best. If Bach's Inventions are played haltingly, without flourish or brilliance and with occasional wrong notes, no great harm is done. They are still very well worth listening to. But imagine Saint-Saëns's Piano Concerto or Cesar Franck's Prelude, Chorale and Fugue badly or hesitantly played. Whatever little appeal these things have would be totally destroyed, their beauty, such as it is, would wholly evaporate. And even if they be played to perfection, I, for

my part, would sooner hear first rate music botched than
second rate music done to a turn.

And so, among the other advantages of the pianola I
would include one that springs from its very shortcomings ;
it serves as an automatic test for the distinguishing of first
rate music from the rest.   The number of admired pieces of
music that fail to stand the test is great.   Let a piece of
music be showy and superficial ; let its appeal depend upon
a tune whose vulgarity is disguised by its complexity ;   let
the theme be too slight for the degree of ornament that it is
made to carry ; let the surface graces and beauties overlay
without wholly concealing the fundamental jejuneness of the
subject, and the pianola will show it up unpityingly, picking out its defects and weaknesses and throwing them into
high relief.

A Bas les Executants.   And so I come at last to the exposition
of my view of what music is and does, a view which the
pianola has done so much to foster.   And lest the prospect
dismay the reader and provoke him to complaint on the
score of irrelevance, asking what all this has to do with the
pleasures of the self, let me appease him by the assurances (*a*)
that the dissertation will be brief, (*b*) that the exposition of
views and theories *is* one of the pleasures of my self, private
in its nature though public in its effects, and (*c*) that I
propose first to divert him and to lead up to the theory by
some preliminary remarks about executants and performers.
among whom I include singers, pianists, conductors and
interpreters generally, which are neither academic nor
agreeable.

The pianola teaches the comparative unimportance of
the *rôle* of the executant.   Indeed, it contrives to suggest
that the executant is something of an intruder.   For me, the
music is the thing.   Hence what I want is the music com-
municated with as little interference or distortion as possible.
It is Bach that I desire to hear and not Bach as interpreted by
Miss XY with her light-boiled "ego" swimming about in a
saucepan of temperament to be cracked by the piano and
swallowed by the public.   All too often the main function of

Miss XY is to interfere with the processes of communicating and receiving the musical "thing in itself". Her inflated temperament is like the crackling noise that interferes with the reception of the music that I hear on the radio. Out, therefore, upon Miss XY, down with her, and give me for the rendering of Bach some little dried-up schoolmaster with spectacles and no temperament worth speaking of to obscure the pane of glass through which the music comes to me. The highest praise that can be given to the interpreter is Pericles's praise of women in the speech which he delivered at the end of the first year of the Peloponnesian war, that they should be least spoken of for good or ill among the men. For my part, I don't want to think about interpreters, I don't want to talk about them or to hear talk about them, and I don't want to be able to distinguish one of them from another.

Technique? But adequate technique is something that one ought to be able to take for granted. A competent pianist ought, that is to say, to be able to play well enough not to arouse comment or attract attention. We are justified in asking for no less ; we are entitled to ask for no more—in a general way, of course.

The Exceptions. For when one comes to particular cases, one must admit that there are exceptions to the generalisation. There are cases in which the art of the executant is so outstanding that it enhances the music, enabling you to hear more in it than you have heard before, to discern in the pattern of the sounds more passion and more beauty and to find more scope for your understanding, sympathy and appreciative delight. Schnabel playing Beethoven is one such case. He invests the sonatas with a wholly new authority—there is really no alternative to this almost meaningless word—almost, one would say, he adds something. (But "adds" isn't after all the right word, since what he brings out is something that was present potentially, there, as it were, all the time, waiting to be actualised by the insight of the great executant.) So, too, Casals can ravish your senses by the sheer beauty of sound. Hear him, for example, playing the Beethoven 'Cello Sonata, Op. 69. The sound of the 'cello is laden with such beauty that it tears at the vitals of your being, so that you are almost driven to cry for respite, like the man driven beside himself by the delicious torture of sexual refinements. But these cases are so rare as hardly to necessitate the withdrawal of the generalisation that the virtue of the executant is the virtue of the Victorian child, that he should be seen but not heard.

The Actor. The actor, in my view, is in the same case. Acting is the lowest of the arts and should not be allowed to intrude the personality of the player between the audience and the play. Competent acting which adequately fulfils the author's intention in regard to his play is something that we should be entitled to take for granted. Actors should be seen and heard only so much as is necessary for this purpose ; beyond that they should not draw attention to themselves.

Cult of Personality. These views are, of course, very far from being shared by my contemporaries. If the concert advertisements are any guide, most people appear to go to a concert to hear not a piece of music but its executant. For the current notice, while printing in the largest letters the name of the star performer, bestows the humblest of lettering upon the music which he is to perform. Sometimes it leaves out the music altogether, so that you are bidden to attend a concert by Miss X, "the celebrated soprano", or Mr. Y, "the famous pianist who will perform 'a number of well-known works' " without being told what it is they are to perform. "I've been to hear Toscanini" or Beecham or even Malcolm Sargent "conduct" says the lady, and proceeds to gush over his exquisite tempo or whatever it may be, without deigning to mention, if, indeed, she knows, what it was that was being conducted. Over pianists and some fiddlers the spate of customary gush is worse. So, too, she will tell you that she is going to the theatre to see Gielgud or Richardson or "Larry", not *The Importance of Being Earnest*, or *Henry IV, Part II*.

This cult of personality is fundamentally unmusicianly. Knowing that it is for them and not for the music that the audiences attend, pianists deliberately cultivate mannerisms and eccentricities of interpretation so that audiences shall have something to know and remember them by. Pachman used to chatter, Mr. X mops and mows, while Miss Y marks her composers by the colour of her frocks. There is the lady rebuked by Enesco for playing the music too fast in order to show off the virtuosity of her technique ; and the scarcely less familiar lady who plays the music too slowly in order to indicate the depth of her feeling.

Cadenza. The apogee of the executant's importance, the summit of his inflation, is reached in the cadenza. I suppose that Beethoven and Mozart wrote their cadenzas to pander to the personality-hunting, sensation-demanding audiences of their own day. And, for the most part, sorry affairs they are, excrescences imposed upon the music rather than growths developing naturally out of it, as an architect may deliberately construct a decoration instead of being moved to decorate a construction. The cadenza lowers the tension, holds up the development and breaks the continuity of the piece. Since, after all, they *are* by Mozart and Beethoven these bravura passages can't help on occasion being glorious, for example, the cadenza to Beethoven's first Piano Concerto, or that wonderful blending of violin and viola in the cadenza to the first movement of Mozart's Sinfonia Concertante. (And is there not a cadenza which Beethoven wrote to one of Mozart's piano Concertos—the D Minor is it, or perhaps the C Minor ?—whose contrast of style invests it with the greatest musical interest ? I shouldn't have had the wit to notice it myself, but when somebody had told me of it, I flattered myself that I could detect the work of another hand.)

But taking them by and large, the cadenzas even of the masters are poor affairs and when, as all too often, the pianist insists on introducing a cadenza by one of the moderns or, worse still, one of his own, the thing becomes an outrage. One doesn't, after all, go to a Mozart concert to hear music by Liszt or Max Reger.

Now the pianola player is at least free from the temptation of personality-mongering. His concern is to render the music as scored by the composer and to render it with as little interference as possible. Just as excellence in the cooking of good meat consists in preserving and bringing out its natural juices so that it may be served without condiments or sauce, the function of the cook being confined to letting the meat speak, as it were, for itself, so the best music requires no interpretation ; it requires simply to be played and this precisely is what the pianola does. How disconcerted Bach would have been by an "interpretation" of music, which he left to speak for itself, by a performer too showy, an orchestra too numerous, in a concert hall too large, as part of a concert too long—four Brandenburgs for example, as I have heard them, one on top of the other ! Most of his clavier music should be played in the conditions appropriate to chamber music, that is to say, in a large room or a small hall by unobtrusive, un-limelighted performers, and it is to these conditions that the pianola rendering approximates. Nor do I think that he would have minded the transcribing for piano or even for orchestra of some of his organ preludes and fugues, and I am eternally grateful to Evans that he should have bequeathed to me no less than thirty-five organ pieces in the shape of rolls cut for the pianola.

The Pleasures of a Piece of One's Mind

I am conscious that this chapter is already over-long. Much of it, I fear, may have been wearisome to the reader, more particularly the description of the anatomy of the pianola, but it has been delightful to the writer, and if it again occurs to you to wonder what all this talk about executants has to do with the pleasures of the self, I retort that this is my book and not yours—at any rate, it is written for my pleasure and the writing of this chapter has been one of the keenest pleasures of the self. I have long wanted to put down upon paper what, over the years, I have come to think about music and the interpretation of music.

But though my pleasure in writing these things has been great, it is as nothing to the pleasure of saying them. There is no less of pomp and pretentiousness and pedantry among the professors of music than among the professors of anything else. What marks the pianists give themselves, what airs they assume because they have acquired a little digital dexterity ! They forget that most piano playing is, after all, only a specialised form of gymnastics and that compared with the gym instructor, the average pianist is quite well paid. Certainly gym instructors aren't taught or permitted to think so highly of themselves because by dint of constant practice they have brought certain parts of their body to a certain pliability and nimbleness and are skilled in displaying their tricks. The better pianists are comparatively immune from this posturing. "Mr. Samuel," I once heard a lady say to Harold Samuel at the end of a concert, "you play so divinely that I think the very soul of John Sebastian must have entered into you." "That, madam," replied Samuel, "is no doubt what makes me so fat." "Madam," I say in the same vein, "you performed that piece very well. But you should come and hear my rendering of it on the pianola." And then, if she be very crass, I regale her with my dubious and detestable pun, "What sensitivity of sole ! " I exclaim. "Compared with *this*, how crude are the extremities of the finger tips."

And of course she doesn't like it. She thinks I am making irreverent gestures at the holy shrine of music, or poking fun at the great masters in whose steps she so perspiringly follows. But the best of the fun comes when I deliver a lecture on the lines of this chapter to some recognised musical body. Layman as I am, I have lectured several times to musical audiences, at the Royal College of Music, at the Bryanston Music Summer School and to gatherings of music students. My lecture has been largely devoted to emphasising the comparative unimportance of the functions for the performance of which the students are so assiduously preparing themselves. I explain to them about the pianola. I point out that a really good pianola—the instrument, I insist, is capable of almost unlimited development—is better than a moderately good pianist. It is not merely, I tell them, that it can surmount all technical difficulties ; of more importance is the fact that it obviates the intrusion of a third personality between the listener and the composer whose work is to be enjoyed—the intrusion, in fact, of themselves.

For the music, I explain to them, is the thing and it is at once their business and their excellence so to soft-pedal their personalities that they may be absorbed in the general creative process. Soft-pedalling their personalities doesn't mean wearing a differently coloured dress to fit the music you are proposing to play, still less changing your dress between the items. All, I say, I want of *them* is to be as unobtrusive and transparent as possible. As for technique, that I tell them, I take for granted. . . .

I have derived considerable pleasure from the outraged murmurings, rising on occasion to a storm of protest that these very obvious remarks are apt to arouse. Pianists can't be expected to welcome the pianola or to tolerate its being taken seriously. For the pianola blacklegs their trade union, and, if the things that I said to them were *quite* true, would bid fair to supersede them altogether. But of course they are not true, at any rate not quite true, but are neglected half-truths thrown into high relief and given exaggerated emphasis by way of reaction from the undue importance which is today attributed to the *rôle* of the executant. I hope that this reaction of mine is salutary. At any rate it does no more than justice to a grossly neglected aspect of the truth.

But you can't expect executants to like it ; hence, the subtle pleasure which I derive from pricking the bubble of their inflated opinion of themselves and their function. I don't know of anyone else who indulges in just this pleasure —though I deduce from his writings that Neville Cardus shares many of the views here expressed. Hence I am relevantly including this baiting of the pianists among the pleasures, the purely personal and private pleasures of the self.

Theory of Music

I have set this out at length elsewhere and am concerned here only to make such a brief statement as will, I hope, afford some justification for the otherwise dogmatic-seeming utterances to which in the previous pages I have committed myself. I propose, then, to make two points.

Affinity with Chess and Mathematics. First, as I have already said, what matters in regard to music is not so much how it sounds but the way in which it is arranged. Let us suppose that you put down with your finger eight notes at random on the piano. Of the impact of the hammers on the wires, of the vibration of the wires, of the travelling of waves in the atmosphere, of the impinging of these waves upon the membranes of the eardrums in the middle ears, of the ensuing vibrations of the drums, of the complex machinery of the inner ear and of the resultant neural disturbances in the brain, physics and physiology between them can give a fairly full account. And that is all. Strike the same notes in such a way that they form the statement of the theme of a Bach fugue and you can be thrilled to ecstasy. In other words, in addition to the physical and physiological effects, there is now an æsthetic effect. Wherein does the difference between the two cases lie ? Not in the sounds, for the sounds are the same, but in their order and arrangement and in the intervals between them. Now order, arrangement and interval, though they link events in the physical world, are not physical events. The affinity of music is, then, with chess and mathematics in that all three depend for their effect and their appeal upon the presence of factors which are not physical but which are the relations between physical factors. Each in its way bears witness to the existence of another order of reality and of its intrusion into the natural order to which our bodies belong and from which most of our experiences derive.

Hence the importance of art ; it is not for nothing that Plato says in the *Phaedrus* that the Form of Beauty is the only one of the Forms which can be beheld by the soul in this order of existence, can, that is to say, be beheld by a soul which is incorporated in a body. Considerations of this kind afford, I suggest, evidence for the life of the soul otherwise than in the body. It is a curious fact upon which nobody, so far as I know, has commented that music, chess and mathematics are the spheres, and the only spheres, of the infant prodigy. It is as if when these gifted creatures came into the world, they brought something with them, brought, in fact, what Plato would call a recollected knowledge of the combinations and patterns that they had known in the real world in which the soul previously dwelt and which is its true home. For this knowledge which they appear to possess cannot be accounted for by experience of this world, since as yet they have had no experience. What is more, intercourse with the things of this world usually leads to the obliteration of this other-worldly knowledge. It is as if some memory gradually became obscured by the events and experiences of ordinary life. Usually, but not always ; there are cases such as those of Mozart, of Capablanca and of the mathematician, Poincaré, in whom the recollection seems never wholly to fade.

This leads to my second point that the emotions aroused by music are not such as belong to and proceed from this world ; or rather, the emotions which music can *distinctively* arouse are not those which so belong and proceed.

Literary Music

Let me explain. Music can arouse a great variety of emotions such as are also aroused by life—melancholy and joy and tenderness and sentimentality and self-pity and an overpowering exaltation of the spirit. What is more, music can arouse these emotions in a glorified form so that they appear to be significant and edifying. As you listen, you drift into a variously coloured day-dream in which, carried away on the waves of sound, you see yourself in a thousand glorious and ennobling situations, leading lost causes, rescuing imprisoned maidens, boldly revenging yourself upon or extending Christian forgiveness to those who have wronged you, staging edifying death-bed scenes for the express purpose of displaying magnanimity to your repentant enemies gathered about your bedside. Or you may make good resolutions, decide to be a better man, to get up earlier in the morning, answer your letters by return of post, pay your bills or be nicer to your wife. Or music may kindle the fires of ambition. Nothing seems impossible to you as you pass from the House of Commons into the Cabinet in order to become Prime Minister, or fight your way through the first three rounds of the singles at Wimbledon.

Some music is especially evocative of the delights of daydreaming. There are certain Preludes and Nocturnes of Chopin for example, which call up in my mind an imaginative picture whose details are vividly etched. It is a dull and broody summer's evening ; twilight is about to fall as, walking through the French windows of the dining room that opens on to the park, I leave behind me the girl I have loved or, alternatively, still love, who is gently weeping on the couch for, indeed, I have just parted from her for ever. The scent of her hair is in my nostrils as I pass out into the still evening and the gently dropping rain. I am filled with a delicious woefulness as I make my way over the lawn to the lake. On reaching the ha-ha, I look back. Somebody has just lighted an oil lamp or, it may be, half a dozen candles in the dining room and I can see the girl's white dress gleaming in their light. Shall I go back ? No ! I summon my reserves of strength and willpower to say "No." But what pleasure, what enormous secret pleasure in this imaginative self-denial ! But was I perhaps not after all resisting temptation ? Perhaps following the mood of the fifteenth Prelude, I was just bored with the woman ? It is so long since I listened to Chopin, that I can't remember.

Most of the music that exists is capable of being listened to in no other way than this—most music and, I suspect, nearly all opera.

I have two comments. First music so listened to is not doing anything for you that literature cannot. Indeed, literature, and particularly poetry, can do it much better. For if meaning is what you want, the meaning that belongs to the things and events of this world and which can, therefore, be expressed, what better medium of expression can there be than words? Even the most expressive music in the world is not so *precisely* expressive as words, which is why most so-called expressive music falls hopelessly wide of its mark, and a piece called *Evening in the Wood* might just as well be entitled *Blast Furnace at Middlesbrough*. (It is also, by the way, why most of what passes for musical criticism, with its talk of musical ethics, the philosophy of music, "the world outlook" of the great composers which the music may be supposed to be seeking to convey and so on, is such utter nonsense. All that really matters about a piece of music is that it should sound well, should, in other words, be beautiful. Who knows or cares what it signifies? Music should have wings, dance, give delight. But if this is what it should do, it is obvious that there is nothing very much to say about it. For there *is* no effect that can be put into words.)

If I am right, one's delight in music is *not* literary; it is a delight in the contemplation of forms or patterns ordered by art. The beauty lies in the ordering and in the patterning rather than in the intrinsic quality of the sound.

Again consider Bach. In Bach's music there is the minimum intrusion of the personal, the minimum appeal to the personal. Who has succeeded, who, indeed, could succeed, in putting the appeal of Bach's music into words. For words were invented to convey the meaning and images of this world. They cannot readily be adapted to convey the meanings and images of another. Which is again why the musical critic who finds himself at home with and easily evaluates what I have called literary music, and has much to say of Chopin or Tchaikowsky, finds very little to say about Bach and Handel and will if he is wise confine himself to severely technical comments.

And when we come to what is obviously mystical music, to the music of the last Quartets of Beethoven, the literary images in which musical criticism deals entirely fail us.

Even from the beginning I knew there was something "phoney" about the kind of account which described Beethoven's music in terms of the struggle of a soul.

Music, then, if I am right, is the window through which man can gain a vision, brief and intermittent, of the real world. It is not a mirror to reflect the temperament of artistes, still less to introduce the listener to the lineaments of the self.

And the emotion we feel for it, that is to say the *distinctively* musical emotion, is the emotion we feel for reality. For the soul being here incarcerated in matter, can view the real only in so far as it assumes material form in sound or paint or stone.[1] In music we glimpse reality at the best through a glass darkly. The excellence of the interpreter is to see that as little of the self as possible is permitted still further to darken the glass.

Some Qualifications

I see that I have put all this with my customary exaggeration, giving greater weight to the element of form in music and making less allowance for the glory and colour of pure sound than a purely objective statement would justify.

But, as I have already hinted, the exaggeration will do no harm if it serves to correct in however small a degree the common exaggeration on the other side. As for the artistes, they can at all times be trusted to look after themselves. Let me, however, do my best to invest my treatment with at least an appearance of impartiality by adding two qualifications.

First, I have said that the pattern or arrangement of the sounds which constitute a piece of music is more important than the sounds themselves ; that, in other words, it is form that counts rather than matter. This is, I think, broadly true. But it is not true in detail, since some sounds, it is obvious, are intrinsically more agreeable than others. And by the word "intrinsically" I mean that they are more agreeable in themselves irrespective of their relation to other sounds and irrespective, also, of whether any hearer or

---

1. The mystics must presumably be excepted from this generalisation.

body of hearers happens to find them so. In view of the contemporary preference for subjectivist modes of thinking in ethics and æsthetics, according to which "this is beautiful" means "I or most people happen to like this", "this is good", "I or most people happen to feel an emotion of approval for this", this statement would require an elaborate defence by way of justification, a defence which cannot be given here.[1] Let me, then, put on record, without attempting to justify, my beliefs, first, that the sounds made by a chorus of cats on the roof are less "beautiful" than the sounds of the second movement of Bach's Double Violin Concerto in D Minor, and, secondly, that this statement is true in spite of the known divergences of taste not only between people living in different ages but also between different people living in the same age. Some sounds, then, are intrinsically more beautiful than others, just as some forms of arrangement are æsthetically more satisfying.

Secondly, although that which excites and moves us in music is, if I am right, unique and cannot, therefore, be described in terms of anything else, there is, nevertheless, one thing that can be significantly said which is that the essence of music is melody. In melody and rhythm, which is part of melody, lie the origins of music. Men danced to rhythms just as errand boys whistle or used, before the era of jazz and swing and crooning, to whistle melodies. Melody is of the essence of folk music. It is melody that catches you, melody that haunts you, melody, then, that you remember. And as music originates in melody so it never completely cuts free from its origins. Throughout the corpus of great music, through the theme of the Bach Fugue, through the movements of even of a Beethoven posthumous Quartet melody runs. Now the outstanding defect in most modern composers is that they simply can't write melodies. Where, to cite only our own people, where in Bliss or Bax or Tippett or Lambert or Scott or even Vaughan-Williams and Britten, will you find a melody which leaps to take possession of your consciousness? It is

1. I have attempted it in *Decadence, a Philosophical Enquiry.*

the absence of melody which makes their music so essentially unrememberable.

Pleasures of the Musical Self

So much for my musical confessions. Now for an attempt to relate them to the theme of this book. There is, first, the pleasure, private and personal, of making the confessions. As I am not a professional musician, my opportunities for writing and speaking about music are very limited. Hence, I have derived an immense enjoyment from putting at last and at length upon paper what after all these years I have come to think. The pleasure of pianola playing itself is also highly private and personal, if only because so few share it.

And the pianola brings its subsidiary pleasures. There is the pleasure of arranging rolls, which is like the pleasure of arranging books, in that it is something that belongs wholly and completely to yourself, something that only you can do.

I suppose that I possess between three and four thousand pianola rolls and they are spread all over the house. About half are arranged, catalogued, labelled and put tidily away on shelves under the names of their composers. Pianola rolls are unwieldy things. They get out of place, they collect the dust, their labels come off, the boxes in which they are housed disintegrate. They afford, then, in high degree all the pleasures of arranging and re-arranging and generally tidying up. Here, for example, are four new Schubert rolls which have been dug up in the Evans jungle and have somehow or other to be fitted into the ground plan of the existing Schubert rolls. This involves altering the position of some thirty rolls of Schubert's, and perhaps making a new arrangement for his chamber and piano music. The alterations may even overlap the works of the next composer who, in my library arrangement, is Schumann. Now the pleasures of tidying up are among the distinctive pleasures of old age, and I enjoy arranging and re-arranging and generally fussing with my rolls.

Secondly, there is the pleasure of exploration. To sit down to a totally unknown piece of music, a Sonata by Haydn or C. P. E. Bach, let us say, without the faintest idea of what it is going to sound like, is a curious experience. You have the feeling of the pioneer voyaging alone on to uncharted seas of sound.

There is, finally, the pleasure of selection. For the most part, as I have explained, I play my pianola first thing in the morning in lieu of breakfast. I generally allow myself two rolls. The first is always a piece of Bach and almost always one of the "Forty-eight". But the second piece ? Shall it be more Bach, comparatively unknown Bach, something newly dredged up from the bottom of the Evans ocean, or something familiar, a movement, say, from a Mozart Concerto ? Or shall I try Cesar Franck or Fauré or Rachmaninoff or even Berlioz, and put myself for the hundredth time to the test of the question, "am I *really* prejudiced in my comparative indifference to anybody but the great six"— Handel and Haydn must clearly be admitted—"or are they," as I should prefer to believe, "in a class by themselves ? "

It will perhaps confirm the reader in his conviction that I am, if I put it on record that I return from these periodic excursions into the musical territory of those whom I call "the others," more particularly if they belong to the twentieth century, convinced that I am not. But the pleasure of being prejudiced and the pleasure of knowing that you are prejudiced and then letting your prejudices rip are among the minor pleasures of the ageing self.